THE ENN[...]

"Nhien Vuong's *Enneagram of the Soul* makes an important and uniquely useful contribution to the Enneagram literature in that she provides a pathway for the types, built around practices and principles to help us apply the system in a deep, yet practical way—so we can really accomplish the spiritual work of transcending the personality."

—BEATRICE CHESTNUT, author of *The Enneagram Guide* to *Waking Up* and *The Complete Enneagram*

"I highly recommend Nhien's compassionate and communal approach to Enneagram work. This book is certain to be a great companion to your growth journey."

—SARAJANE CASE, author of *The Honest Enneagram*

"*The Enneagram of the Soul* is a masterpiece. It is a treasury of wisdom, filled with spiritual insights and practical exercises to help you live a more soul-centered life. I wholeheartedly recommend this book to you!"

—ROBERT HOLDEN, author of *Shift Happens!* and *Higher Purpose*

"*The Enneagram of the Soul* is powerfully potent medicine for self-healing. It is a loving, inspiring, thoughtful, and useful book for those interested in real inner development and having a more deliberate life."

—CATHERINE R. BELL, MBA, founder of The Awakened Company and author of *The Awakened Company*

"I've been using *Enneagram of the Soul* for the last several weeks as a daily reflection and guide for self-observation and I cannot recommend it highly enough. It's clear that Vuong has a deep understanding of the Enneagram born not only of study but of *practice* and *experience;* something many Enneagram teachers are missing. *The Enneagram of the Soul* is an invitation into the practices and experiences that allow you to not only understand the system more fully but also cultivate a loving and compassionate understanding of yourself. This is the perfect companion for anyone who sees the Enneagram as an embodied journey and not just an intellectual pursuit."

—ABI ROBINS, author of *The Conscious Enneagram*

The Enneagram of the Soul

The Enneagram of the Soul

A 40-Day Spiritual Companion for the 9 Types

NHIEN VUONG

Foreword by Russ Hudson

HAMPTON ROADS

To Mom and Dad
who taught me to persevere in love—
just as they have

CONTENTS

PART II
Forty Activations

ACKNOWLEDGMENTS

For the first several decades of my life, I lived under the lie that I came into this world frighteningly alone and irredeemably unloved. If my contemplative journey with the Enneagram has taught me anything, it is that this seemingly inborn truth has been the greatest self-deception of my life—a delusion perpetuated by my Enneagram Type 3 lens, which selects only the data that says,

I am a separate doer.

and

My worth must continually be earned.

I was at first mortified yet ultimately relieved to realize that my decades-old, drama-filled story that "I did it by myself!" and "I do everything myself!" is a myth. In truth, my existence has never been singular. I have done nothing on my own.

With much relief, gratitude, and humility, I give thanks not only to the Divine indwelling but to all the soul family and friends who have faithfully loved me into being—and *becoming*—the person I am today. Because of you, my lifelong loneliness has been crowded out by intimacy, love, and a sense of belonging. Furthermore, I know beyond a doubt:

This is not "my" book. This book exists because of you.

- To my family, my pack (Colby, Effie), and my extended pack (Laura, Barbara), *I love you.*

- To my Evolving Enneagram community and especially my CPE peeps, *I cherish you.*

- To my Founders Circle, *I bow to you*: JoMarie Andrews, the late George Benner, Mary Ann Benner, Angela Joy Johnson, Kristina Frank and Family, Jodi Jackson, Stuart Jackson, Cathy Jolliffe, Pastor Jeff Gannon, Reverend George Gordon, John Greenleaf-Maple, Macha Greenleaf-Maple, Joyce Mosiman, Paul Mosiman, Tom Nye, Nancy Pauls, Patti Regan, Jim Regan, Julie Sahlin, Jan Stanley, Keith Stanley, Carol Wells, Dr. Darrell Youngman, and Trish Youngman. Thank you for believing in my ministry.

To my special friends who pored over the many details of my entire manuscript to help ensure its quality and integrity, *I salute you*: Angela Joy Johnson, John Greenleaf-Maple, and Macha Greenleaf-Maple.

To my literary agent, *I honor you*: D. Patrick Miller, thank you for inviting me to take my first formal Enneagram training over twenty years ago, for encouraging me to be an author, and for helping me to believe in miracles—like the completion of this book!

To my dear Unity, U-Nite, and ACIM communities, *I have traveled far and wide since meeting you, but I carry you in my heart everywhere I go*: Victor James Dougherty, Reverend Robert Brumet, the UIM Board, the UIM Prayer Chaplains, and especially from UIM, Reverend Bill Englehart, Bonnie Aby, Barbara Cochran, Larry Gorski, Darrell Holdaway, Steve Listug, Tom McAuliffe, Helen Sharritt, Sue Silkworth, Pat Tostenson, and Nevin Valentine. Your generosity is something I will never, ever forget.

"We are Groot!"

Good job, everybody!

FOREWORD

It comes as a surprise to many people that the way we look at things is not always as objective as we might imagine. Our way of looking at life and experiencing things feels like reality, yet seldom do we notice how much the particularities of our psyches, shaped by temperament and by our life experiences, filter and shape our perceptions. This is true on an individual level, but also on a collective level. It may be even harder to consider that the ways our current societies see things are not necessarily how they have always been known. Indeed, we need only look at some of the current world cultures different from our own to realize that we human beings have many ways of experiencing the world.

The entry level of studying the Enneagram lies in this—recognizing that our way of being is simply one of many possible ways, and that it is possible to recognize and appreciate ways that are different from our own. While many know only the descriptions of the nine Enneagram types, now becoming widely known, fewer make the leap to the next stage, when we begin to understand why we behave as we do. This is what sets the Enneagram apart from other systems that describe the different manifestations of personality. The Enneagram gets under the surface and reveals many of our deepest motivations and wishes, as well as our most deeply entrenched fears and limiting notions about ourselves. Once we begin to grasp this system at this more powerful level, we begin to understand others better in ways that open up the possibility of real connection and intimacy. In my many years of teaching this work, I have frequently been touched to witness couples, long in partnership with each other, suddenly "get" why their partner behaves as they do. "Oh! That's why you do that!" Such realizations offer new possibilities for us and our relationships. And if what we are studying doesn't do that, why bother?

At its most profound level, the Enneagram, based as it is in spiritual traditions, helps us begin to understand and experience what we are beyond our ego self. And it is in this way that Reverend Nhien Vuong's marvelous book, *The Enneagram of the Soul*, invites us on a journey of profound self-discovery. Many books on the market now can describe the nine Enneagram types with a degree of accuracy that can help readers discern which of these patterns fits them best. But far fewer are the books that help us see what to do with this knowledge.

Reverend Vuong has been diligently studying the Enneagram for many years, but more importantly, she has been engaged in the practices that bring this knowledge to life. Her approach is eclectic, and she has learned from many of the Enneagram traditions and teachings. She guides us into applying the lessons of the nine Enneagram points to the particularities of our daily lives—understanding that the vicissitudes of our lives offer the real and true gateway into authentic spirituality. For me, this is the true purpose of this Enneagram, and the way to best employ its many possible applications.

I would also invite you to be aware of the tone of Reverend Vuong's writing— the voice with which she shares her understanding. You may notice several unusual things. First, while it is certainly true that her information is clear and accurate—she has done her homework, at all points—her tone is invitational and compassionate. She knows what this work is for, what it supports, and how it can help, and she delivers this in a manner that helps us feel understood and appreciated—even when we have to look at the less delightful parts of our personalities! You may also notice that throughout the book, she is consistent in reminding us of the orientation of looking at ourselves with honesty and kindness. This orientation can take us very far in our journey home. And lastly, Reverend Vuong well understands a key concept that George Ivanovich Gurdjieff, the man who brought the Enneagram symbol to the attention of the modern world, emphasized in all his teachings. This is that any real inner work will lead us beyond our culturally conditioned obsessions with self to a realization of our fundamental connection with all of humanity, and all of life. This beautiful book helps us remember that the real and original Enneagram work helps us shed concepts of ourselves and others that no longer serve us so that we may prepare ourselves for the mysterious and fantastic changes ahead—that we all know are upon us. I feel strongly that our future much depends on us human beings discovering how we might truly meet each other beyond our historic beliefs and notions, and when we use the Enneagram in the way this book recommends, we are well on the way to that possibility.

It warms my heart to see how many people across the planet are discovering and embracing the Enneagram, but it inspires me and lifts my spirit to see the rising work of Enneagram teachers such as Reverend Vuong who really do understand what this work is for. I am delighted to be part of introducing *The Enneagram of the Soul* to the world and to welcome Reverend Vuong into the company of guides and teachers who are using the amazing tool in alignment with its original sacred purpose. May you have an extraordinary journey with these pages.

Russ Hudson
Santa Fe, New Mexico
April 14, 2024

INTRODUCTION

Behind the plentiful headlines of bad-news-as-usual, a conscious evolution is taking place on a global scale. More and more people are waking up from the mental, emotional, and behavioral habits that keep us numbed out, preoccupied, internally bankrupt, and disconnected from ourselves, one another, and the infinite ground of being that is variously called God, Divine Love, or simply Truth. As we emerge from the fog of forgetfulness into the light of self-remembrance, we are coming to discover wholeness as our true nature. The recognition and activation of our wholeness in itself enriches our personal lives in meaningful ways, while also seeding and sustaining some of the most potent activism happening on Earth. This contemplative activism pursues justice that rejects othering—not only of any groups of people, but also any parts of our precious selves. These whole-person politics are rooted in love rather than hatred, are informed by wisdom rather than ignorance, and are inspired by faith rather than fear.

Among those seeking liberation from our own petty thoughts, shrunken hearts, and exhausted nervous systems, an increasingly recognizable symbol is being shared across the historical divides of religion, race, nationality, age, and gender. This symbol is known as the Enneagram.

The word *Enneagram* comes from the Greek *ennéa*, which means "nine," and *grámma*, which means "that which is drawn." As depicted in Figure A, the Enneagram symbol is a circle cradling a triangle and a hexagon that, together, touch the circle at nine equidistant points. Each point around the circle's circumference has been assigned a number—9-1-2-3-4-5-6-7-8, in clockwise order from the apex.

The person responsible for bringing the Enneagram symbol to the modern world was an Armenian mystic named George Ivanovich Gurdjieff (1866–1949). Gurdjieff taught the Enneagram as a living symbol that is moving and dynamic. Throughout its history, the Enneagram symbol has been used to chart psychological traits, archetypes, spiritual gifts, the movement of energy, and more. In modern times, in great part due to the pioneering work of Bolivian philosopher Oscar Ichazo and Chilean-born psychiatrist Claudio Naranjo, who brought the Enneagram to the United States, the focus shifted toward personality types, as well as their interrelatedness in terms of Enneagram type–based conflict styles, social styles, and communication styles. The Enneagram has also been used to plot our inner work and spiritual development. Arrows have been

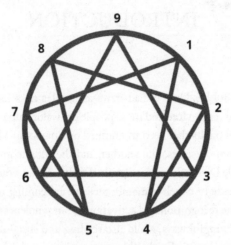

Figure A: The Enneagram

added to many Enneagram depictions to reflect the dynamism and directionality of such processes, whether along the inner lines or around the symbol's circumference. Certain Enneagram maps are descriptive and others are prescriptive, mirroring the most beautiful and troubling aspects of the human psyche. The scope of this mapping is dazzling, and many resources exist today that explore its intricacies. Some of my favorites are listed in Appendix B.

My primary intent in writing this book is not so much to add to the abundance of wonderful Enneagram teachings (although I hope that this book will do some of that). My main purpose is to offer a practical, Enneagram-informed inter-spiritual companion guide to support fellow wisdom seekers in applying this symbol's remarkable powers to their everyday lives. This book is intended especially for those of you whose spirituality, like mine, doesn't fit into a particular religious box. Rather, your spirituality thrives on curiosity, openness, and wonder. It focuses on *embodying* a dynamic love and mystical truth rather than on consensus around a prescribed dogma or belief system. Specifically with respect to the Enneagram, I seek to support you in living out your own unique answers to these two questions:

I know the Enneagram. So what?

and

I know my Enneagram type. Now what?

As you take this inward journey, my deep hope is that you experience more fully the exquisite presence, power, and purpose of your own soul and, in doing so, contribute to the inside-out healing of our world.

The Enneagram of the Soul is inspired by over two decades of my inner and outer work with the Enneagram, which is ongoing. Over these years, I have had the honor of spiritually mentoring individuals, couples, families, and business partners from diverse social, cultural, and faith backgrounds around the world. I have been blessed to have the opportunity to teach the Enneagram to corporate executives, physicians, teachers, therapists, social entrepreneurs, Enneagram professionals, pastors and other spiritual leaders, as well as to the incarcerated and those in addiction recovery programs, among countless others. I have been profoundly enriched by my work consulting and counseling on matters related to caregiving, grief, transitions, and death. For the past seven years, I have led multiple weekly contemplative Enneagram practice and support groups dedicated to community-based, compassion-centered transformation, and I have facilitated contemplative Enneagram intensives and retreats around the world.

I've been studying the Enneagram since 2002 and teaching it since 2007—primarily from a Unity perspective.[1] Unity teaches an allegorical rather than a literal understanding of the Bible—one that holds that all beings are in truth whole, perfect, and sacred, irrespective of their race, background, sexual orientation, gender identification, or belief system. Though there are now Unity churches around the world, Charles and Myrtle Fillmore, who cofounded the movement in 1889, intended that Unity's spiritual teachings be shared with individuals of all faiths as well as non-faith backgrounds, affording each person freedom to learn and practice Unity principles within their own religious or nonreligious contexts. Foundational Unity principles are that love, wholeness, goodness, and oneness are the unalterable essence of *all* that is, including *you*.

When I discovered Unity in 2004, I was a Stanford Law–trained attorney. In 2012, I left the practice of law and mediation in the San Francisco Bay Area to pursue a calling to serve the evolution of consciousness. This took me to the Greater Kansas City Area for seminary, and I have lived in the Midwest ever since. An ordained Unity minister since 2015, I focus on faith, not as a matter of belief, but as a lived, embodied experience of love, wholeness, and unity. I am deeply honored to be an Accredited Professional with Distinction (APD) with the International Enneagram Association (IEA), which strives to ensure a level of depth, experience, and ethics among the ever-expanding cadre of self-professed Enneagram experts. (To date, fewer than thirty Enneagram professionals in the world hold that mark of distinction, which is reserved for "IEA members who have attained a level of advanced knowledge and experience in using the Enneagram within their designated professional field and/or for teaching Enneagram."[2])

My Enneagram training is extensive yet also diverse. I am a Certified Somatic Enneagram practitioner and mentor, as well as a Certified Enneagram coach through the IEA-Accredited Awareness to Action Program. I formally trained with Claudio Naranjo's legendary Seekers After Truth (SAT) teachers in their SAT1 program in 2019 (sadly, just days after Naranjo passed away). I have also studied at length with The Narrative Enneagram (TNE) since 2006. One of the two oldest Enneagram schools in the United States, TNE was cofounded by Helen Palmer and David Daniels and was the first Enneagram school in the US to earn the label "IEA Accredited School with Distinction." I have learned much from other master Enneagram teachers, whether through their books or online and in-person trainings, including the legendary Russ Hudson, A.H. Almaas (the pen name for the founder of the Diamond Approach to Self-Realization, Hameed Ali), Katherine Chernick Fauvre, Robert Holden, Peter O'Hanrahan, Helen Palmer, and Sandra Maitri, to name but a few of the Enneagram giants on whose shoulders my work rests.

Today I work primarily under the umbrella of my own business, Evolving Enneagram, that I founded in 2019 upon leaving church ministry and through which I serve as a hub for an amazing group of kind-hearted, free-spirited Enneagram collaborators who are focused on transforming lives using a whole-person, compassion-based approach to the Enneagram. My outer work, which is currently focused on the spiritual dimensions of the Enneagram, is deeply informed by my own living, breathing, and meditating on the sacred implications of the Enneagram—this *mandala of wholeness*—infusing it into my own journey of awakening for the past twenty-plus years.

> *The Enneagram is, at its most abstract, a universal*
> *mandala of the self—a symbol of each of us.*
>
> —Don Riso, Enneagram author and cofounder of
> The Enneagram Institute

Waking Up with the Enneagram

My Enneagram initiation occurred on a remarkably cloudless day in July 2002 in my one-bedroom rental apartment in San Francisco at one of the lowest points of my life. Earlier that week, I had given notice at my corporate law job, asked my husband for a divorce, and moved out of the home we had purchased only months prior. I had just enough savings to live on for six months in that expensive location, no real friends (aside from a few former colleagues), a large family from which I was both emotionally and geographically distant, and zero plans for what came next.

Naturally, I did the only thing I knew to do back then. The one life-giving, hope-lending activity that had nurtured me through my profoundly lonely childhood was reading. So, I acquired a stack of books—all "self-help" books—and dived in.

One of those books was about the Enneagram. The book referenced an online Enneagram personality typing test called the RHETI,[3] so I quickly took that test the same morning. I scored highest as a Type 3, with Type 1 coming in a very close second. At that time, the descriptions I read for Type 3 (which I later discovered to be my actual type), did not fully resonate with me. When I read the descriptions for Type 1, I wept for a solid afternoon.

My tears tasted of both grief and hope. What had cracked my poised and arguably "cold" lawyerly exterior wide open was the teaching about Ones' (who identify as Type 1) need to be right. That characteristic felt embarrassingly true for me. My next thought was to call my soon-to-be ex-husband to apologize—which I did—because it must have been unbearable to live with someone who believed she was invariably right and, moreover, was often righteous about it. Even more significantly, however, I learned that day that the Ones' compulsion to be right—and, ultimately, to be *perfect*—is driven by a core limiting belief that they are fundamentally wrong or bad.

Whoa! What? That really hit home, because the underlying question that had plagued me since as far back as I can remember was: *What's wrong with me?*

Most people who knew me then would have been surprised to learn about this deep insecurity. To all appearances I was living the American Dream as a native Vietnamese girl who had been evacuated by a military plane out of a war-torn country in her infancy. I spent my formative years sharing a small, three-bedroom house with nine others: my mom and dad, three grandparents, and four siblings—a multilingual, ethnic Vietnamese, and Buddhist household—in the predominantly Caucasian, politically conservative, Protestant town of San Clemente, California. I excelled academically, graduating from Stanford Law School—one of the top three law schools in the nation at the time—and then became a well-paid San Francisco attorney at a prestigious San Francisco Bay Area law firm during the turn of the century's dot-com boom. I was married to another Stanford Law alum, and we owned a home in one of the nation's most sought-after places to live.

Accomplishments aside, I had always strived to be what I considered a "good" human. It mattered to me—and continues to matter deeply—that I be impeccable with my word, respect my elders, give my time and talents generously to those in need, operate ethically and with integrity, and work hard with devotion and dedication. My father worked as a janitor at first and eventually as a chemical engineer at the local sewage plant, my mom and two grandmothers did odd sewing jobs to support the family, and my grandfather shelved books at the public library. From my early elementary years well through my college years, I volunteered at senior and convalescent homes and hospitals, coordinated food drives, and much more—often leading the charge for these community service activities.

Given my life circumstances, one might have had reason to think that I had a legitimate basis for feeling good—or at the very least remotely okay—about myself. But as far back as I can remember, I believed that something was terribly wrong with me. I didn't feel at home within myself or in the world. From my earliest years, I had felt like a foreigner, even in my own family, a fraud in my schoolwork and career, and certainly my own worst enemy as I corrected, bullied, and berated myself into obsessive self-improvement, hoping that one day I would earn the right to love—or at least *like* myself.

If that sounds like a nightmare, it *was*.

Fortunately, the Enneagram's appearance in my life jostled me awake to the notion that there was an underlying reality I was not perceiving because of the limiting lens through which I saw the world. For the first time, I started to challenge not just my behavior but my perception, which impacted everything else about my life. More specifically, I was beginning to wonder:

What if the only thing "wrong" with me is that I believe that something is inherently wrong with me? And how would I live differently if I knew I am already whole and perfect exactly as I am?

We Teach What We Most Need to Learn

I later hit an even lower bottom, finding myself in twelve-step recovery, and then discovered the wisdom teachings of *A Course in Miracles* (ACIM) along with the radically loving and inclusive framework of Unity spirituality. More than twenty years after discovering the Enneagram, it is clear to me that the gift I want to share here is one I have deeply needed in my own life.

More specifically, three autobiographical themes shape this book. First, as I mentioned earlier, I was a profoundly lonely person for the first three decades of my life. As a little girl, it was through books that I found my first sense of kinship in this seemingly cold and alien world. Decades down the line (and far from traveling a *straight* line), I have finally come to experience deep and authentic compassion for myself—a sense of inner hospitality, wholeness, and belonging within my own existence.

Second and not unrelatedly, through my Enneagram soul work, I have come to feel my interconnectedness with all life. I began to shift into a feeling of connection, unity, and even sweet friendship with all that once felt so very foreign and strange. Along this journey toward greater belonging, I came across the term *anam cara*, an expression popularized by the Irish poet-philosopher John O'Donohue. *Anam cara* essentially means "soul friend." I delighted in this idea even as I was developing a deepened appreciation for how engaging in spiritual practice with support and guidance from mentors and community transformed me in a way that no self-help book alone ever could. I realized I didn't just need self-help or self-care. I needed community-help and community-care. I didn't just need to receive it. Nor did I need to just give it. Rather, I needed to engage life as an integral part of it—to share in it, and thus, to both give and receive care.

Finally, the term *little* plays a big role in this book's conception. I stand at a towering five feet, two inches. Throughout my life, I've affectionately been called "little" by many, and my life partner often refers to me as a "little person with big energy." It makes sense then that the first book I'd ever write is a little book that wants to be your *anam cara* on the Enneagram journey of realizing your wholeness and your sense of intimate belonging and unity with all of life. You will, I hope, come to know this not by my personal testimony but by *your* own life experience:

The deepest things that you need are not elsewhere.
They are here and now in that circle of your own soul.

—John O'Donohue, *Anam Cara*

HOW TO USE THIS BOOK

This is a little book with big dreams. It wants to sit by your bedside and offer on-the-spot consolation when you are grieving. It wants to fall into your day-pack and show up on top of the mountain you just climbed. It wants to be the voice that challenges your limiting beliefs and skewed vision and urges you to *Look! Then look again!* This book wants to go to work with you and remind you there are (at least) nine fundamentally different vantage points from which to see and solve the same problems.

This book is premised on the reality that we are *not* just our Enneagram personality types. The sheer dynamism of what we truly are is much larger, less definable, and much less predictable than each of our own type-based inner narratives would suggest. Furthermore, when we live from an awareness of our wholeness, we experience a greater sense of inner peace, purpose, and fulfillment. A companion guide, this book intends to steer you gently yet firmly away from the trap of identifying with your personality so you can live more and more from your divine nature. This includes operating less from the filtered, limiting, and fixated lens of your Ennea-type and more from a freedom to experience reality in its stark and immense beauty.

As you begin this book, whether alone or with others, keep in mind that it is not meant to be consumed in a single sitting (though you are free to do so)! *The Enneagram of the Soul* is intentionally broken down into bite-sized morsels meant to be savored and digested slowly—and, if possible, among the company of family, friends, and fellow spiritual seekers.

In terms of how to progress through this book, you might wish to start at the beginning and read the pages in order. Alternatively, you might feel guided to simply open randomly to a page and see what message jumps out at you. Chances are you will do a little of both. I recommend that you trust your own inner wisdom. If you are new to the Enneagram—or curious about my spiritual, whole-person approach to it—you might wish to peruse the Enneagram primer included herein. Know, however, that this book is set up so that you can *ideally* open it anywhere and get something out of it, regardless of how much you know (or don't know) about the Enneagram. Furthermore, if you do not already know the Enneagram, I hope you will quickly recognize its power to transform your consciousness and thus your life.

This companion guide has two main parts followed by two appendices. In Part I, I set forth *nine principles* to guide your journey of transformation using the Enneagram, *nine practices* to propel and sustain the transformational process, and *nine prayers* to lend heart to your journey. Part II offers *forty activations*, which consist of very brief questions, reminders, or practices, on forty different themes customized for each of the nine Enneagram personality types. The reflection questions at the end of each activation can be used either alone or by a study group. The activations are meant to be reflected upon and applied one day at a time or, depending on your preferred pace, one week at a time for a total forty-day or forty-week journey. You can repeat the journey as often as you would like and witness how much has changed (or remained consistent) since you last practiced the same activation. *Appendix A* provides guidance for group facilitators and participants wanting to work through this book together. *Appendix B* lists a bibliography and recommended resources for those interested in learning more about the Enneagram or engaging in a multinational, inter-spiritual, Enneagram-literate community.

A PRIMER ON THE
ENNEAGRAM OF THE SOUL

Our type, awakened or asleep, remains the same.

—Sandra Maitri, *The Spiritual Dimension of the Enneagram*

My aim here is not to stake a claim to some Ultimate Truth about the Enneagram; my intention is much more pragmatic and, I pray, also more poetic and inspirational. My hope is to offer you Enneagram kindling for the fire of your soul. In my experience, poetry, metaphors, and symbols all ignite the soul far better than a list of categories and definitions. So, let's start with a few reflections on the Enneagram symbol.

The Circle: A Symbol of Wholeness, Unity, and Oneness

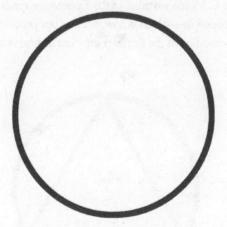

Figure B: The Enneagram Circle

The Enneagram symbol is said to be derived from sacred geometry, which suggests a kind of mathematical patterning to all of existence. That the Enneagram image is encompassed by a circle (Figure B), then, is not incidental but intentional—and profoundly meaningful. The Enneagram circle is said to represent a spiritual law: *the Law of One.*

When I reflect on this circle, I am reminded of the intrinsic wholeness of all of life, and not just my individual wholeness but the fundamental wholeness of everyone and everything. Thus, I cannot accept the gift of wholeness in a vacuum—that is to say, I cannot accept *my* wholeness while rejecting *yours.* Nor can I somehow accept our collective unity—that is, embrace the oneness of all life—while exiling parts of myself.

When I look at the Enneagram circle, I see a reflection of our universal wholeness and collective unity. I also recognize, however, that, even among those of us who believe that oneness is the underlying essence of reality, on the surface, separateness and disharmony seem to hold sway as inevitabilities of our human condition. This is where the symbolism of the inner triangle becomes helpful to consider.

The Inner Triangle: A Representation of the Fall into Ignorance and the Path for Our Conscious Awakening

Inscribed in the circle of the Enneagram is an inner triangle linking points 9, 6, and 3, as shown here in Figure C. When we think of the Enneagram symbol not as merely representing nine "types" of people—which is how much of our popular culture these days circumscribes our understanding of the Enneagram—but instead as representing one whole

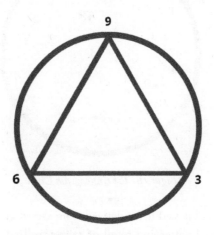

Figure C: The Inner Triangle (9-6-3)

individual, we can view the qualities represented at points 9, 6, and 3, and the movement between those points as mirroring aspects of our own inner worlds. More specifically, translating the writings of Enneagram authors A.H. Almaas and Sandra Maitri through my own Unity perspective, I see the movement from point 9 to 6 to 3 as representing what Christians might call the fall from grace or what the Buddhists might refer to as the fall into ignorance.[4]

Point 9, which sits at the crown (or top) of the Enneagram symbol, can be seen as representing the initial loss of contact with our divine nature. This movement away from undifferentiated oneness serves as the foundational basis of ego development or individual selfhood. Notably, from my Unity perspective, this movement is not actual but only perceptual—that is to say, becoming human means coming into an *experience* of separateness. In this, at point 9, we lose conscious awareness of our intrinsic wholeness and oneness with Spirit, God, or the Divine (by whatever name we call the Infinite), yet our wholeness and oneness remain intact. In Maitri's words, "instead of experiencing ourselves as unique manifestations of one thing . . . we come to experience ourselves as ultimately separate, and thus cut off and estranged from the rest of reality."[5] This results in a state of emptiness at our core—again, not limited to people who identify with Enneagram Personality Type 9, but universal to us *all*, as symbolized by point 9 on the Enneagram, viewed as a map of consciousness.

Next, point 6 on the Enneagram can be seen as representing the existential anxiety, reactive alarm, and even primal terror that arises from the perceptual loss of contact at point 9. At point 6, we drop into the sense of being minuscule relative to the enormity of all that is *not* us—exposed and vulnerable beings existing within but distinct and separate from the totality of life, including what some of us might call God. To the extent, then, that we believe in a god, it *appears* to be "out there."

Finally, point 3 on the Enneagram can be seen as representing our response to that existential threat. More specifically, we fashion one of nine basic identities around that response—and eventually forget that this self is a construct rather than the whole of our true, divine nature. This forged identity is our Enneagram personality type, which might also be called our *persona* (derived from the Latin word meaning "mask"). Our type, then, is not who we are in truth; rather, it is simply how we have shaped and conditioned ourselves to best survive. Additionally, the more we habitually (and most often unconsciously) react from this conditioned self, the more entrenched our fabricated identity becomes and the further we get from the dynamism of our natural, open, authentic state of being.

The path from 9 to 6 to 3 can thus be seen as representing the human condition—of having "fallen asleep" to our oneness with Spirit, Truth, or Reality. When I spiritually mentor individuals and groups, I reference this central triangle to map our way home—from point 3 back through our terror at point 6 then finally to a state of blissful union at point 9. In short, spiritual awakening can be seen as a path of *communion*, or a coming back into union—not in fact, but in consciousness—because, again, at least from a Unity perspective, separation only happened in our (highly subjective) perception.

This path of communion—the path of conscious awakening—begins, then, at point 3 (aka the false self) in all of us. This is metaphorically where all nine Enneagram personality types (or the nine personas) live. This is why even though this book is explicitly *not* about the Enneagram of personality, the forty activations I offer here are tailored to each of the nine personality types. When we more clearly perceive the obscurations and limitations most characteristic of our personality type, we can embrace our wholeness by willingly and intentionally stepping outside the mental, emotional, and behavioral patterns that orbit our respective types. Additionally, the nine practices offered in this book are designed to strengthen the muscle of letting go of those habits of type and to be compassionately present to whatever feelings or experiences arise within us as all the limitations and sufferings of our persona become clear to us. As we allow ourselves (and others) to witness the constructed nature of our sense of self, this makes space for the light of our dynamic wholeness to infuse our conscious awareness and thus our real-life choices.

If you do not already know your Enneagram personality type, you will soon learn that the process of discovering it is a thrilling, albeit deeply humbling, journey of realizing how the radiance of your soul is imprisoned. Appendix B includes resources for supporting you in this artful discernment. Another tip is that the forty activations in this book that are tailored for your type will not necessarily feel desirable, comfortable, or easy for you. These activations endeavor to meet you where you are in your type—while also inviting you to take on challenges to offset the fixation of type, which includes certain habits of attention, feeling, and behavior that might feel normal or natural to you but that are simply ingrained habits of your personality.

In *The Seat of the Soul*, Gary Zukav wrote: "Every decision that you make either moves you toward your personality, or toward your soul." We can live either from the defended reactivity of our point of suffering or from the fount of creativity that flows effortlessly from our inner, essential light.

From Personality to Individuality

By definition, soul evades the cage of definition. It is the indefinable essence of a person's spirit and being. It can never be touched and yet the merest hint of its absence causes immediate distress.

—David Whyte, *The Heart Aroused*

The Enneagram of the Soul is about discovering what you truly are, all that is possible for you, and what is hopeful for our world when each of us loosens the chains of our fixated selves and unleashes our imprisoned splendor. This is not about prescribing what your unique soul-splendor should look like, nor is it about demonizing or rendering evil, bad, or sinful any part of yourself (including the ego) as some religious traditions might attempt to do. To the contrary, this soul journey is about embracing our personality as a part of our wholeness. The main issue with the personality is not that it is inherently bad or wrong; it is simply not the totality—the full grandeur—of your being. When you are identified solely with your personality, you end up living from the mere surface of your self—a life devoid of Spirit and of soul. (See Principle 1: You Are Not Your Type.) In contrast, living from individuality is about living from the ground of being that is your spiritual or core nature. Conceptualizing this from an Enneagram perspective, you might understand living from your individuality to be living from your dynamic essence, living from the center of your Enneagram circle (i.e., being centered in Spirit), and letting that nature radiate outward—rather than living from your Enneagram point on the circle's circumference and revolving your life around this seemingly separate sense of self. Again, we need not shame ourselves for living from a separate sense of self. (In fact, I find that it is unhelpful to shame ourselves for pretty much anything.) In this case, it is simply about realizing and remembering that, to the extent that any of us over-identifies with our personalities, we suffer from the distress of our separation from the Divine. We also suffer from the type-driven quest to grab from the world whatever we think we need to be at peace, to feel worthy, to experience joy or satisfaction—while never feeling content with what we find. When we realize our mistake, we can gain much relief, release, and rest from all that futile seeking! The misdirected seeking of the personality is aptly illustrated by the ancient parable of the Sufi teacher known as Nasrudin:

Nasrudin's friend Mansour comes to visit him and sees Nasrudin on his hands and knees, crawling on the sidewalk under the streetlamp, obviously searching for something and appearing frustrated.

Concerned, Mansour asks, "Nasrudin, what are you looking for? Did you lose something?"

"Yes, Mansour. I lost the key to my house and I'm trying to find it, but I can't."

"Let me help you," responds Mansour. Mansour joins his friend, kneels on his hands and knees, and begins to crawl on the sidewalk under the streetlamp, searching. After a time, having looked everywhere on and around the sidewalk, neither Nasrudin nor Mansour can find the lost key. Puzzled, Mansour asks his friend: "Nasrudin, where did you lose the key? When did you last have it?"

"I lost the key in my house," Nasrudin responds.

"In your house?" repeats the astonished Mansour. "Then why are we looking for the key here, outside on the sidewalk under this streetlamp?"

Without missing a beat, Nasrudin explains, "Because there is more light here!"

The key to our soul's fulfillment was never lost outside, in the world, but in our house, within our own consciousness. To the extent that we follow the habitual tendencies of our Enneagram type (sometimes shortened to Ennea-type), we will continue looking for our key out in the world where there seems to be more light. Only when we stop looking outside and become willing to brave some of the darkest parts of our inner terrain will we ever come to know the fullness of our being—and see with an inner light beyond our wildest imaginings.

Who looks outside, dreams; who looks inside, awakes.

—Carl Jung, Swiss psychiatrist and psychotherapist

According to Sufism, each soul enters the world with a special sensitivity to one particular aspect of this inner, universal light. The Enneagram traditionally names these lights the *Holy Ideas*. These Holy Ideas are not just intellectual concepts; I prefer to think of them as the nine faces of God or, better yet, as Hameed Ali (whose teachings on the Holy Ideas serves as a foundation for my own here) calls them, "facets of Unity."[6] If Reality is seen as pure consciousness, which is how my Unity spiritual tradition sees the Divine, then these ideas are literally facets of that consciousness.

Enneagram Personality Types

Following are brief descriptions of the nine Enneagram personality types as reflections of the nine faces of God or Divine Mind. May these serve as helpmates on your journey of embodying your own inner light—a journey undertaken not only for yourself but for our aching world.

You are the light of the world.

—Matthew 5:14

Enneagram Type 1
(OFTEN CALLED THE PERFECTIONIST OR REFORMER)[7]

Out beyond ideas of wrongdoing and rightdoing,
there is a field. I'll meet you there.

—Rumi, Sufi poet and mystic

Those who identify as Type 1 possess an inborn talent for bringing order to chaos. They tend to be highly conscientious, ethical, and self-controlled individuals. They are especially gifted at perceiving the ideal potentials and organizing structures for everything around them, including themselves, which can lead to perpetual frustration as they see others not working nearly as hard to better and, ultimately, to perfect the world around them.

Ones are said to enter this life with a particular sensitivity to the Holy Idea of *Holy Perfection*: that is, the experience of everything being whole, right, and perfect just as it is. The One's personality type structure seeks to compensate by fixating the One's attention on whatever appears imperfect and then working dutifully (and often compulsively) to correct, reorder, and otherwise perfect it. Thus Ones take on a habitual posture of standing against whatever *is* (including themselves), in favor of their internal ideal regarding how things *should be*. Thus, personality-fixated Ones live under the tyranny of a harsh inner critic that punishes them when anything falls short of their ideal. As a result, they feel the weight of the world on their shoulders—a self-imposed burden made even heavier by righteous indignation and resentment toward those who never seem to take on their fair share of responsibility for fixing everything.

As Ones begin to wake up, they experience greater serenity as they learn to feel at peace with people and situations exactly as they are. Soulful Ones release their insistence on one "right" way to see, believe, and behave, and start to see the world less in terms of black-and-white oppositions and more in terms of the colorful spaces in between. They start to appreciate the naturally occurring beauty, elegance, and goodness in all people and things. As they become less harsh, judgmental, and critical, they naturally become more humane and joyful. As their presence becomes less demanding and faultfinding, they become *more* likely to inspire others to take responsibility for realizing their highest selves; thus, soulful Ones no longer feel the need to carry all the burdens of the world by themselves. Centering in their own wholeness, awakening Ones are increasingly wise and discerning. While living for a purpose beyond themselves, they know clearly not only what skillful actions they need to take but also what attitudes or action to refrain from, what to let go of, and where it is ideal to let people or situations simply be.

Enneagram Type 2
(OFTEN CALLED THE HELPER OR THE GIVER)

> *Generosity is giving more than you can,*
> *and pride is taking less than you need.*

—Khalil Gibran, Lebanese-American writer and poet

Those who identify as Type 2 are naturally empathetic, caring, friendly, and demonstrative. They tend to value their significant relationships above all else—and often wish those they love felt the same way. Twos habitually focus on attending to others' needs while often not recognizing or valuing their own.

Twos are said to enter this life with a particular sensitivity to the Holy Ideas of Holy Will and Holy Freedom, which together form a direct experience of one will operating freely and unconditionally for the good of all. Bereft of the connection to this universal will, Twos not only feel unloved and unsupported, but they also feel compelled to proactively take on the task of supporting their "special somebodies" in an often-unconscious effort to get their unacknowledged needs met—"giving to get."

Being needed becomes a substitute for being loved. Twos can be so entranced by their own efforts, they come to believe with some pride that others are, in fact, very much dependent upon the Two's help, support, praise, flattery, and encouragement. Behind this pride, however, is the Two's sense of humiliation and shame (often unconscious) around even *having* needs or wants of their own. This can sometimes lead to desperate efforts on their part to get their legitimate needs met through possessiveness or manipulation, such as by using flattery, seduction, or people-pleasing, even while they believe they are acting only in the interest of others, never themselves.

As Twos begin to wake up, they experience true humility: an awareness that allows them to acknowledge that they, like all humans, have important needs and desires. Additionally, soulful Twos recognize that they sometimes need help and, out of newfound love for themselves, they are willing to risk the pain of rejection to ask for it. Centered in wholeness, maturing Twos recognize that there is only one universal will, unfolding for the good of all. This enables them to become unconditionally giving, humble about their genuine place in other people's lives, more receptive to experiencing the sincerity of others' love, and more heartfully focused on their own joy, spontaneity, and nurturing. More conscious Twos learn to enjoy solitude and often their own creative pursuits. They recognize that sometimes the greatest gift they can give others is the gift of their own being and receiving.

Enneagram Type 3
(OFTEN CALLED THE PERFORMER OR ACHIEVER)

Soul, if you want to learn secrets, your heart must forget about shame and dignity. You are God's lover, yet you worry what people are saying.

—Rumi

Those who identify as Type 3 are born with an aptitude for efficient and productive action that readily attunes and adapts to an ever-changing world. Threes tend to be hardworking, efficient, and pragmatic—they are able to set aside their feelings to get tasks speedily accomplished, only to confuse what they do and the image they project for who they genuinely are.

The Type 3 personality structure derives from a sense of being disconnected from the Holy Ideas of Holy Hope and Holy Law—the universal principles that allow us to experience how the universe and all things within it operate according to natural and immutable laws (and that no effort or interference on our part is needed for this to be true!). Moreover, Threes can hope for the best without taking full responsibility for making it happen themselves. Not trusting in life's natural progression, Threes compensate by making things happen, believing that if anything worthwhile is going to happen in this world, they need to *personally* make it happen. Threes also tend to believe that they are self-made—that they are solely responsible for constructing their own inner (and outer) world. Under the paradigm of a growth mindset, they focus attention on fashioning themselves into the kind of person they think will be most admired—which varies according to context. They focus on performing whatever roles they've assigned themselves with efficiency and excellence in a hamster-wheel effort to prove their worth. In this way, personality-fixated Threes stay busy performing and image-crafting, while disconnecting from their hearts so they can steer clear of a gnawing inner sense of worthlessness.

As Threes begin to wake up, they become more honest with themselves about who they really are and what they truly want. Their outer expression more closely matches their inner state and authentic desires. Cultivating more self-acceptance and inward focus, they come to know themselves apart from what they make, achieve, accomplish, or do. Correspondingly, soulful Threes become more transparent (especially to themselves), more compassionate (including with themselves), more patient (with everyone), and much more able to laugh at life (and particularly at themselves). Awakening Threes experience a sense of their intrinsic value—which can open from within like a precious pearl. Thus, they feel less of a need to strive to earn a sense of value in the world. Relatedly, they also become better at taking pleasure in life, genuinely appreciating and valuing their relationships and everyday experiences. Centered in their wholeness, Threes naturally become more genuinely modest, collaborative, and charitable.

Enneagram Type 4
(OFTEN CALLED THE INDIVIDUALIST OR TRAGIC ROMANTIC)

You are not a drop in the ocean;
You are the entire ocean in a drop.

—Rumi

Those who identify as Type 4 are born with a great sensitivity to the world, along with an immense capacity for feeling and a nuanced attunement to life's beauty and its depths. Fours tend to be highly creative and expressive, with a flair for the dramatic. They often focus on what is missing and on their own sense of longing for what is unavailable. They habitually compare themselves to others, feeling either uniquely inferior or exceptionally superior, and can prefer their own fantasies to everyday life, which can seem all too superficial or banal.

The Four's personality type structure suffers from a perceived loss of connection to the Holy Idea of Holy Origin, which allows us to sense how everyone and everything are deeply connected; in fact, we all emanate from the same original source. Fours compensate for this feeling of disconnection by attempting to mimic *origin-ality*, crafting a specialness they paradoxically believe will entitle them to "belong" again. They're not necessarily aware of this melancholic longing and tend to believe they were born to stand apart and that their distinctiveness and sensitivities are both the blessing and curse of their existence, causing them to suffer more than others—sometimes quietly and other times with intense hostility. Their habitual attention to what makes them unique—and, in many cases, uniquely tragic—only takes them farther from the truth: *that they never separated from Holy Origin.* Mired in sadness and shame from feeling abandoned, fixated Fours enact a special kind of suffering, which keeps the cycle of bittersweet nostalgia and their idealization of what is unavailable alive.

As Fours begin to wake up, they develop a greater sense of equanimity. They are less subject to the whims of their moods and do not need to exaggerate or dramatize their experiences to feel special; consequently, they live with more self-renewing inspiration. Soulful Fours develop a taste for the exquisiteness of everyday joys—experiences that they may have previously regarded as overly pedestrian or mundane. Their attention stabilizes better in the here and now, and they fantasize less about another more idealized time or place. As they begin to forgive life (or themselves) for not being anything other than what it is (and what they are), they give themselves permission to feel the satisfaction of both having and being enough in the here and now. They recognize that, spiritually, they have never been abandoned and that nothing essential is missing. Centered in their wholeness, Fours often become balanced, disciplined, and creative in ways that express not only their personal truth but also overarching, universal truths.

Enneagram Type 5

(OFTEN CALLED THE OBSERVER OR INVESTIGATOR)

Open your hands
If you want to be held.
—Rumi

Those who identify as Type 5 are born knowledge seekers with an immense capacity to focus on and develop complex ideas and skills. They tend to be inventive, innovative, and private, and prefer to maintain the perspective of a detached (and thus, in their minds "rational") observer rather than a fully engaged participant in what appears to be an unnecessarily messy and depleting human existence.

The Five's personality type structure bears a perceived loss of connection to the Holy Ideas of Holy Transparency and Holy Omniscience, which together offer us the awareness that the universe is fundamentally one—One Mind with its infinite multiplicity. Although we recognize how we are unique differentiations of that Oneness, we also experience boundaries between us as truly "transparent" (we are differentiated yet utterly inseparable from all that is). Disconnected from this awareness, Fives feel severed from life—incapable of participating in its abundance. Far from transparent, the boundaries between themselves and others look more like castle walls! Consequently, when fixated, Fives rigidly defend against the pain of isolation and fear of rejection by becoming exceptionally self-reliant and guarding against incursions on their personal resources, which might include their space, time, or privacy. At an unhealthy extreme, they can become cynical and detached observers (often critics) of life rather than fully engaged, heartfelt participants.

As Fives begin to wake up, they experience a greater sense of inner knowing, trust, and healthy non-attachment (as opposed to reactive detachment). They become more able to observe themselves and others without judgment or expectations. They take brave and bold action to partake in the rich experiences of life, share their competencies with the world, and embrace the messiness of human relationships. Soulful Fives become visionaries and thought leaders who are privy to an infinite universe of knowledge, comprehending the world not only with their heads, but also with their hearts and bodies. This connection to a deeper *gnosis* ("direct knowing") and inner prosperity makes space for them to be with the mysteries of life. Centered in their wholeness, Fives generously share their resources—especially their own heart, presence, and vision.

Enneagram Type 6
(OFTEN CALLED THE LOYALIST OR THE SKEPTIC)

Once the seed of faith takes root,
It cannot be blown away,
Even by the strongest wind.

—Rumi

Those who identify as Type 6 are born troubleshooters who seek a sense of security while habitually doubting whether or where that security might be found. They are great problem-solvers and team players. They can be immensely loyal to the people or causes they believe in as well as vigilant and heroic in protecting themselves and those they love from harm.

The Type 6 personality type structure is formed in reaction to a perceived disconnection from the Holy Ideas of Holy Faith and Holy Strength, which afford us an experience of Spirit as the eternal, infinite ground of being that provides us with a sense of strength and certitude that we have what it takes to meet an ever-changing and uncertain world. Missing this deep inner reassurance, Sixes compensate by becoming hyper-attuned to dangers and hypervigilant in their quest for security, stability, and certainty. Compulsively looking outside of themselves to find ideas, systems, or people to trust only distances them further from their own inner knowing. This can lead the Six to feel increasingly reliant upon external sources—whether it be rules or a protective authority, group, or teacher—to guide and support them. Once a Six has chosen to trust an external source, they feel compelled to meet the expectations of that particular person or organization; this sense of loyalty further fuels their tendency to overthink, steering them further from their intrinsic guidance. Divorced from their own center of security, Sixes second-guess themselves. This includes struggling to trust any source they find, including the authorities on which they most seek to depend. When fixated in their type, Sixes live with chronic self-doubt, indecision, worry, and caution—and sometimes reactivity and defiance—as they struggle to feel confident in their choices and relaxed enough to thoroughly enjoy life.

As Sixes begin to wake up, they start trusting in an invisible yet felt ground of being within themselves as their true, abiding source of support. Consequently, they become more self-affirming, internally stable, self-reliant, and trusting of others. Equally important, they come to trust their own inner guidance. While they are natural team players, soulfully centered Sixes become more confident leaders at home, at work, and in community. They can not only anticipate potential problems, but also bring in positive and faithful thinking, spectacular wit, and light-heartedness to bear on all challenges. Centered in their wholeness, Sixes are beacons of courage that light a path in the dark for us all.

Enneagram Type 7
(OFTEN CALLED THE ENTHUSIAST OR EPICURE)

How will you know the difficulties of being human, if you are always flying off to blue perfection? Where will you plant your grief seeds? Workers need ground to scrape and hoe, not the sky of unspecified desire.

—Rumi

Those who identify as Type 7 are born with quick wits and highly charged nervous systems that seek constant excitement, variety, and stimulation. As a result, they tend to stay busy, especially mentally busy, quickly jumping from one entertaining idea or experience to another like a rock skipping over the surface of water. Because they deeply fear pain and limitation, they struggle to stay in the present moment and make space for difficult feelings—their own as well as others'. Further, Sevens can fear they'll stay stuck in any negative emotion they allow themselves to feel.

The Seven's personality type structure is developed from a perceived loss of connection to the Holy Ideas of Holy Wisdom, Holy Work, and Holy Plan, which together allow us to experience life's organic unfolding and transforming. In other words, the Holy Work of our lives, which can only ever happen in the present moment, proceeds, moment by moment, according to a wonderfully wise plan or design. Disconnected from this knowing, Sevens compensate by adopting an enthusiastic, scheming mentality of *I'll make sure it happens.* "It" usually refers to something the Seven has deemed positive, pleasurable, or desirable. It is less about committing to one plan than it is about ensuring avenues for future good. Indeed, when operating from their fixation, Sevens seek to ensure limitless possibilities to avoid being trapped in pain by thinking ahead, planning for grand adventures, and keeping their options open—just in case any chosen path begins to feel dreary, boring, negative, or unproductive. They tend to compulsively seek the rush of new ideas or experiences, struggling with anything that would threaten to restrict their freedom. Those perceived limitations may well include others' rules, feelings, or relative slowness.

As Sevens begin to wake up, they sense their unlimited place in the natural progression of life, trusting that their joy is an integral, spontaneous part of that unfolding. They experience the virtue known as *sobriety*, which enables them to savor the fullness of the present moment without the need for diversions or exciting secondary plans. Soulful Sevens become fully present to the whole spectrum of human life, including the full range of negative and positive feelings. Centered in their wholeness, Sevens assimilate experiences in greater depth, with their hearts as well as their minds, while sharing their awe, enthusiasm, and appreciation for all the wonders of life in the here and now—a gift that bubbles over to us all.

Enneagram Type 8
(OFTEN CALLED THE BOSS, THE PROTECTOR, OR THE CHALLENGER)

> There is a sacredness in tears.
> They are not the mark of weakness,
> but of power.
> —Rumi

Those who identify as Type 8 are typically born with vast energy, confidence, decisiveness, and a willingness to fight for what they believe in. Eights can be fiercely independent and seem controlling to others when mostly they are simply making sure that *they* are not being controlled. They get fired up in the face of injustice and are instinctively protective of those they deem innocent and vulnerable and whom they believe are being taken advantage of.

The Eight's personality type structure is formed in reaction to a felt disconnection from the Holy Idea of Holy Truth, which despite appearances, is an experience that, in truth, all is one: *there is only one reality for us all, one existence that is here, happening right now.* In response, Eights adopt a defensive us-versus-them mentality: a belief that the world is somehow against them, with life being no more than a constant battle, whether for resources, love, or belonging. They develop an armored self that identifies with power, fights for justice on the proverbial battlefield of life, struggles with moderation, and denies any weakness or vulnerability within themselves. The fixated Eight's reaction to almost any difficulty is reflexive anger—which they readily express. Not typically conscious of their own weaknesses or dependencies, they can run themselves to the ground before recognizing the value in admitting to any powerlessness or vulnerability.

As Eights begin to wake up, they increasingly connect to a more innocent, childlike view of the world as undifferentiated Oneness—they no longer have to separate themselves from a hurtful world. Their hearts soften and they engage life with greater vulnerability, gentleness, open-heartedness, mercifulness, forbearance, and benevolence. Always a helper and often a protector, their way of giving shifts from powerfully doing *for* others to sharing more and more heartfelt space *with* others. Soulful Eights use their ready, abundant life force for the greater good. Centered in their wholeness, Eights develop a capacity to slow down, to make more space for others to step in, to help, and even to lead. No longer led by the need for "bigger" or "more," they become more self-disciplined and self-regulating, which enables them to burn fewer bridges, achieve longer-term visions, and become even more authentically powerful and heroic.

Enneagram Type 9
(OFTEN CALLED THE MEDIATOR OR THE PEACEMAKER)

You must ask for what you really want.
Don't go back to sleep!
. . . The door is round and open,
Don't go back to sleep!

—Rumi

Those who identify as Type 9 have a natural gift for seeing and embracing all perspectives and being energetically attuned to their environment. They tend to move instinctively away from conflict, drama, or discomfort, seeking instead places and situations in which they can feel peaceful, comfortable, and harmonious. This can lead to complacency, inertia, and neglecting to speak their truth or fulfill their calling.

The Nine's personality type structure is rooted in a sense of disconnection from the Holy Idea of Holy Love—the awareness of the radiant loveliness of all beings, including themselves. The Nine's style of compensation is the "urge to merge," whether with comforting foods or routines, beloved others, or their social milieu—to narcotize themselves from the pain of feeling unlovable and insignificant. They adopt a pattern of "self-forgetting," in which they distract themselves from their own inner world and priorities. At an extreme, this self-forgetting can show up as physical or emotional self-neglect as Nines unconsciously avoid the inevitable shame and despair they would feel if they directly faced their deeply held sense of being insignificant. As part of their overall avoidance strategy, Nines invest their social energy in being accommodating or unobtrusive, seeking to maintain outer harmony and avoid conflict. Fixated Nines can tend to make idols of comfort, peace, and harmony, even as they fall into a deeper and deeper sleep around their own inner truths, feelings, or desires. This can lead to sporadic outbursts of anger as Nines unconsciously rebel against their own passivity and lack of caring for self.

As Nines begin to wake up, they recognize that their inner worlds *do* matter and begin to courageously express their uniqueness, even when it might result in discomfort or disharmony. Recognizing their own significance, they naturally become more alive and engaged in life. They become more self-possessed and proactive in asserting themselves. Soulful Nines learn to prioritize their personal goals and dreams and are even willing to brave the spotlight as needed to express their truth. They feel more substantial, exercise their innate power, and relish their sense of autonomy. Centered in their wholeness, Nines are a powerful force of nature and bring their gift of seeing and of embracing all perspectives, including their own.

The Enneagram of the Soul: One Path Among Many

Whether my perspective on the Enneagram is meaningful or helpful is, of course, entirely up to you to determine. I believe that none of us should take anyone's views, including our own, as gospel without trying them on to discern for ourselves what is true and to ferret out the untruths we might have unconsciously been living with for years. Ultimately, if the Enneagram does anything for us at all, it should remind us that there are *at least* nine fundamentally different perspectives on life, all equally valid from a vantage point that is grounded in the depths of our soul, that is, at the center, rather than on the mere surface or circumference of self where we habitually sit on the Enneagram circle. My hope is that this book nurtures you in finding and walking—and perhaps sometimes skipping or even crawling, if you need to—toward wholeness, along your authentic path of soul.

Say not, "I have found the truth," but rather, "I have found a truth."
Say not, "I have found the path of the soul."
Say rather, "I have met the soul walking upon my path."
For the soul walks upon all paths.
The soul walks not upon a line, neither does it grow like a reed.
The soul unfolds itself, like a lotus of countless petals.

—Kahlil Gibran

PART I

Nine Principles,
Nine Practices,
Nine Prayers

NINE PRINCIPLES

*We can only accept teachings that we have put
into practice with our own awakened understanding
and that we can see with our own experience to be true.*

— Thích Nhất Hạnh, *No Death, No Fear*

Following are nine principles to ground and guide your journey of conscious awakening using the Enneagram. May each serve as a helpful touchstone. If you find an idea foreign or challenging, I invite you to give it a test run rather than simply adjudicating its rightness or wrongness intellectually. Consider trying on each principle by living or acting as if each is true to see what impact doing so might have on your everyday life and, more specifically, on the way you apply the Enneagram to living with greater authenticity, purpose, and soul.

Principle 1: You Are Not Your Type

*Discovering your personality type is merely the trailhead
to a deep, complex, and important journey to self-discovery.
It's the place we start, not the place we end.*

—Drew Moser, *The Enneagram of Discernment*

Let's begin our journey with this fundamental principle: You are not your type.

Indeed! You are *not* your Enneagram type. You might identify with your personality style, but who you are in truth is not a personality. You might operate regularly from ego, but you are not your ego. You might routinely default to certain attitudinal habits, fixations, or compulsions characteristic of your type, but nevertheless, you, in essence, can never be defined or limited by any of these.

We are not human beings having a spiritual experience. We are spiritual beings having a human experience.[1] Granted, you may have fallen asleep to your true nature simply as part of the journey of *becoming* human. You, like most of us, might even need regular support to stir your wakefulness and to help you to reawaken day to day or even moment to moment (very much a part of being human). But what you—what we *all*—are in truth is *spiritual* and thus infinite and eternal. Incarnated into this life in original blessing, you are also, at the core, whole, perfect, and inseparable from all of life.[2] Your true nature is indescribably exquisite, loving, dynamic, and radiant. Remember this and remind yourself of this often, even as you continue to deepen in your Enneagram journey toward embodying your wholeness. The subtlety of this distinction is crucial to live your way into: you may have a type, but you are not your type.

What you think you are is a belief to be undone.

—*A Course in Miracles*

Principle 2: Your Type Is a Gateway to Spiritual Freedom

You are in prison. If you wish to get out of prison, the
first thing you must do is realize that you are in prison.
If you think you are free, you can't escape.

—Gurdjieff, Armenian philosopher and mystic

If you are not your Enneagram type, then why learn about your type at all? First, learning the common characteristics of your type helps you to recognize the prison walls within which you habitually—and mostly unconsciously—live, thus supporting you in becoming more conscious and ultimately free. More specifically, the Enneagram helps you to see type-based patterns of feeling, thinking, and behaving that are your type's core compulsions. It aids you in seeing how these patterns, which you have tended to think are simply (and perhaps even irrevocably) "me," reflect only a partial, idealized version of you. Relatedly, discovering your type helps you recognize the various ways you have become over-identified with this limited self-image and have shut out or disowned parts of your wholeness that do not support this persona. Through this reclamation of repressed or exiled attributes, the Enneagram empowers you to realize your full, divine potential.

Discovering your type can help further a sense of belonging. It helps you to normalize your life experience and thus supports you in feeling less alone in the world. You realize, often with amazement, that others share a similar way of approaching life, and, with that, a similar set of gifts and struggles. Some have joked: "Others of my type share my brand of crazy!" Discovering how your type crosses historic lines of race, gender, culture, religion, and nationality is often profoundly healing as you discover similarities between individuals who have come from backgrounds quite different from your own. Often, learning the Enneagram typology helps the world make more sense and feel smaller, more interrelated.

Finally, knowing your type matters not merely as a point of entry into greater wholeness and belonging, which is found at the center of your being, but also as a point of reentry into more creative and fulfilling life expression as you begin to live from the inside out. Remember that even as you evolve, you do not ever change your Ennea-type. You simply become more liberated and less fixated in how you relate to your point on the Enneagram map of consciousness. You begin to express more of the underlying virtues and gifts of your type. Knowing your Enneagram type thus helps you to live your higher purpose and potential in this life. As you begin to awaken to the truth of your inmost being, the light that you are radiates out through your core point on the Enneagram in a way that can only be described as a soul-splendor. And this is what it means, after all, to live the Enneagram . . . of the soul.

> *There is an inmost centre in us all,*
> *Where truth abides in fullness*
> *. . . and, to know,*
> *Rather consists in opening out a way*
> *Whence the imprisoned splendour may escape,*
> *Than in effecting entry for a light*
> *Supposed to be without.*

—Robert Browning, extracted from "Paraclesus"

Principle 3: Type Is Rooted in Motivation, Not Behavior

What are you trying to do [is] one of the easiest
to ask and most difficult to answer of questions.

—Robert K. Greenleaf, *Servant Leadership*

One of our deepest unconscious patterns is the
false belief that we already know ourselves well enough
to understand why we think, feel, and act the way we do.

—Beatrice Chestnut, *The Complete Enneagram*

Enneagram type is based on our core motivation and not our behavior. To illustrate, two individuals might work hard to become successful CEOs of Fortune 500 companies for quite distinct reasons. For instance, an Eight might seek the position to maintain a sense of power, dominion, or autonomy—or perhaps to create a big impact while not letting others control or impact them. Deeper down, they might come to realize they are protecting a part of themselves that feels innocent and vulnerable, in the context of a world that appears harsh and that crushes the weak. A Three, on the other hand, might seek the same CEO role to feel accomplished, gain a sense of worth, or elicit respect and admiration. Deeper down, they might come to realize their efforts to curate image and garner prestige are attempts to feel valuable because they do not feel they are worthy by being their genuine selves.

Different people can step up to help their favorite Enneagram teacher at a workshop for very different reasons. A Nine might do it because they have merged with their teacher or class and enjoy participating in a sense of shared mission and purpose; alternatively, they might be sensing a disturbance in the room that they instinctively seek to remedy so they can feel more at ease. Deeper down, a Nine might come to realize that behind wanting to feel comfortable or peaceful is a fear of confronting their existence, a fear that their personal existence does not matter. A Two might proactively help their teacher, even before asking whether help is needed, because they want their support to stand out, please, and win them favor with the teacher. Deeper down, they might come to realize that behind the need to help is the fear that if they are not needed, they will be unloved, rejected, and abandoned.

While certain motivations can often lead to common behaviors, tallying behaviors deemed typical to a type without considering the underlying reason for those behaviors can lead to mistyping. In contrast, making the effort to uncover the main, underlying reason you tend to do (or not do) something is key to discovering type. This inquiry process can take considerable time and patience, as your core motivation is often not the most obvious reason you did something; rather, it is often subconscious and buried beneath more surface, initial answers.

As you more deeply reflect on the question of motivation, it is important to be kind and compassionate with yourself. Consider, after all, how people are less likely to open up to a judgmental person than they would to a nonjudgmental friend. In my experience, when people struggle to find their type (or, like me, initially *mistype*) it is often because we would be self-condemning if we admitted certain aspects of ourselves *to ourselves*.

On discovering your type, Franciscan priest Father Richard Rohr famously comments, "If you don't sense the whole thing as somehow humiliating, you haven't yet found your number. The more humiliating it is, the more you are looking the matter right in the eye."[3] This is not to say everyone who discovers their type necessarily feels shame or humiliation. However, in my experience, most people, even the most cheerful and positive Sevens, sense that something is being named about them in their Ennea-type that they would rather keep under wraps. Self-compassion and self-acceptance are helpful not only to facing our truth but to truly seeing ourselves in the first place. Keep digging then, even when it feels unnecessary, hard, or boring. Uncovering your core motivation is worth it because you, dear reader, are worth it!

Inquiry into our core motivation is important not only in discovering our type but in opening to a freer, more soulful existence. After all, as we begin to recognize the core motivation that has driven our entire lives, we realize the extent to which even our greatest egoic efforts have proved futile. Rather than despair, however, we can celebrate this disillusionment for what it is: the beginning of awakening to truth. Stubborn as the ego is, many of us do not start this inner quest for wholeness until we have emotionally and often physically exhausted ourselves pursuing all other avenues—until we finally come to learn, for example, that for each of our types,

No amount of
perfecting or correcting (e1),[4]
supporting or seducing (e2),
accomplishing or image-crafting (e3),
dramatizing or fantasizing (e4),

researching or compartmentalizing (e5),

worrying or preparing (e6),

ideating or pleasure-seeking (e7),

challenging or protecting (e8), or

accommodating or self-numbing (e9)

can ever get us the experience of

divine perfection (e1),

unconditional love (e2),

intrinsic worth (e3),

authentic connection (e4),

compassionate wisdom (e5),

steadfast faith (e6),

deep satisfaction (e7),

playful innocence (e8), or

blissful union (e9).

According to the wisdom teachings of *A Course in Miracles*, when we are looking through the eyes of the self that believes it is separate from Spirit, we seek and do not find. This is because what we seek already belongs to us in truth, but it is not *out there*. As painful as the disillusionment can be from our worldly striving, it is eventually replaced by a sense of fulfillment from the inside out.

Everything we need is already here. From within, we claim more of our wholeness not only as our divine inheritance but as our gift to the world. We get here by asking ourselves not just What *is it that I repeatedly do?* but also Why *do I do this?* Asking only *what* can keep us focused on behavior. Asking *why* can take us to our core.

And you? When will you begin that long journey into yourself?

—Rumi

Only when compassion is present will people allow themselves to see the truth.

—A.H. Almaas, American writer and spiritual teacher

Principle 4: Enneagram Memes Can Keep the Bigness of You Stuck in Little Me-ness

*The Enneagram doesn't put you in a box. It shows you the box
you are already in without realizing it, and the way out of it.*

—Russ Hudson, Enneagram scholar and coauthor of *The Wisdom of the Enneagram*

*God is always bigger than the boxes we build for God, so
we should not waste too much time protecting the boxes.*

—Richard Rohr, *Everything Belongs*

Enneagram memes are popular these days. While these memes can sometimes be quite hilarious and brilliant, too often they are simply pithy statements, stereotypes, or caricatures that attempt to define you by a group of behaviors common to your type. Those memes are helpful to the extent that they help you to see—maybe for the very first time—many of your type-based patterns. But when we get overidentified with the memes, repeatedly saying to ourselves and others *"Hey! That's me! That's me! That's me!"* we can get even more deeply entrenched in our egoic Enneagram grooves. In essence, the meme says: "Here's your box!"

The main point in recognizing and naming our patterns is to help us to break free of those patterned behaviors, to figuratively *get out of the box*, as the preeminent Enneagram teacher Russ Hudson has been exclaiming to Enneagram students for decades. Naming our common Ennea-type behaviors can be a useful and even vital starting point for those of us seeking to become more self-aware. However, it can devolve into an unproductive egoistic loop when all we do is talk about what we are, do, or tend to do (yes, even when speaking disparagingly of ourselves). Little space is made in that case to transcend the limiting patterns of our types or to acknowledge how those patterns might be harmful to ourselves or others.

For instance, take the many Type 1 memes that tend to emphasize how organized or exacting Ones are or how lazy the rest of the world is by comparison. Such memes only reinforce the stereotype of Ones as being perfectionistic or overly responsible. They don't encourage Ones to get messy and be playful, for example, which are key behaviors to embracing their wholeness. Additionally, many Type 4 memes that emphasize how unique or long-suffering Fours are do not inspire individuals of that type to feel gratitude for the here and now of everyday life. Fours are left in the prison of keeping up their internal or external drama while maintaining fantasies about what others have that they still lack. Further still, Sevens who find themselves laughing at, creating, or even posting all the clever memes that emphasize how much Sevens can be the charismatic life of the party are only reinforcing their underlying fear: "it is not okay to not be okay."

These are just a few examples of how Enneagram memes, when cliché and over-used, can keep the vastness of you—and all that you are capable of being—stuck in little me-ness. After all, so much of the soul's journey hinges on your ability to release your identity stories and reclaim those shadowed aspects of yourself that you often (even subconsciously) refer to as "not me."

Notably, there are also many funny cat memes these days, some of which depict cats preferring to play with their gift boxes rather than enjoying the gifts within. There is certainly nothing wrong with boxes per se. Exploring the packaging your spiritual gifts come in may be fun, cool, and interesting—but don't forget that an even better gift is inside: the gift of your authentic selfhood.

Neglect not the gift that is in thee.

—1 Timothy 4:14

Principle 5: We Inter-Are

"To be" is to inter-be. You cannot just be by yourself alone.
You have to inter-be with every other thing. This sheet
of paper is, because everything else is.

—Thích Nhất Hạnh, *The Heart of Understanding*

Imagine a world in which we all treat ourselves and one another as equally worthy. We are not only self-compassionate but compassionate toward all of life. Our loving-kindness encompasses the whole of existence—not because a spiritual teacher or text says we should but because *love* is what we truly are. I believe that it is possible to cocreate such a world. Moreover, the Enneagram can be a core component in helping each of us to realize that we *inter-are*; thus, to love our neighbor is to love our expanded selfhood, the greater whole of who (or what) we are in truth.

One major challenge we face on this journey of realizing our unity and oneness is that, particularly in the Western Hemisphere, the self-help industry overplays the rugged individualist paradigm. The same can be said of the term *self-care*, which became a mainstream mantra in the 2010s and has since been described as the gentler cousin of the highly disciplined self-help ideal. Both concepts have the same flaw: they focus *only* on improving and nurturing *you*—with no mention of how your individual healing and wholeness are inextricably joined with the healing of the larger community, and vice versa.

To be clear, focusing on individual healing isn't bad or wrong. In fact, it is an essential step to the journey of awakening. It reflects an important shift from outer-directed seeking to a more inner-directed quest for fulfillment—a seeking that is designed not to idolize our personality (the part of us that believes it is a separate self), but to point us toward our soul (which radiates our unique expression of oneness from the inside out). Very often, a primary barrier to this process is confusing navel-gazing and ego-obsession with the deeper journey described earlier in the Enneagram primer—the daring adventure of leaving the fixation of our point on the Enneagram's rim and venturing into the fuller circle of our wholeness.

Wholeness, I maintain, is not individual. But neither is it anti-individual. It seems that as we travel to our depths, we arrive at a place within ourselves that is awake not only to our individual wholeness but also to our fundamental unity and interconnectedness with all of life. Our movement toward an all-inclusive compassion—and active care for the earth and other beings—is a *natural* expression of remembering who we are. The shift between "I" and "we" is less like bridging a chasm between self and other and more like performing an ancient dance around a sacred fire, a dance in which we sometimes link arms and sometimes let go—but we can never dance our way outside the Enneagram circle of wholeness.

> *God is a circle whose center is everywhere,*
> *and its circumference nowhere.*
>
> —Empedocles, *Empedocles: The Extant Fragments*

Principle 6: We Cannot Awaken in Isolation

We are born in relationship, we are wounded in
relationship, and we can be healed in relationship.

—Harville Hendrix, *Getting the Love You Want*

We need one another. This is not to say that we are necessarily dependent on one another. Nor are we truly independent from one another. Rather, to use the term coined by Stephen Covey in 1999, the reality of existence is that we are *interdependent.*[5] Whereas Principle 5 highlights the underlying *spiritual* truth of existence (we inter-are), Principle 6 focuses on the *worldly* implications of that truth: we cannot awaken by ourselves. As Gurdjieff is famously reported for having told his students: "It's not just difficult to do 'the work' alone; it's impossible."

This is quite a conundrum for many of us. Too often, we may find that the very individuals or communities we most want or expect to support our spiritual quests are the very people who seem to obstruct our way—even ostracizing us for taking this path. As a result, many of us feel lonely, unseen, and without adequate guidance.

Inner work accompanied by a trusted teacher or mentor along with engagement in a conscious (ideally Enneagram-literate) community are essential to realizing our innate wholeness and authentic belonging. After all, self-observation is a key component in spiritual awakening; and if we're being honest with ourselves, most of us struggle to see ourselves clearly. We need other people to hold up a mirror not only to our fixations and delusions but also to our innate divinity, lovability, and the gifts that we might not readily notice in ourselves. We need others to offset the perceptual biases of our type's lens so we can witness life from all perspectives—around the circle of individual wholeness and collective unity that is represented by the Enneagram symbol.

Compassion and acceptance from ourselves and from others are so vital to our development! We desperately need safe spaces among people who are also devoted to this work with whom we can interact regularly—to practice operating outside the respective idealizations of our types in a deliberate and committed way. This is especially true given that we are likely to face an internal backlash when we stray from our type structure. Often, we can experience resistance within our relationships as well. Even the most well-intentioned friends, coworkers, and family members may feel threatened as we refuse to show up in old, habitual ways that no longer serve our highest good. In an Enneagram-literate conscious community, we "get it" if you are a Two who is practicing saying "No" for the first time, a Nine who is struggling to assert yourself, a Seven who is learning to stop running and to grieve for the first time, a Four beginning to embrace authentic joy, a Three or an Eight who is practicing slowing down, a One or a Six who is opening to more spontaneity and play, or a Five who is learning to embrace the messiness of expressing feelings. When we undertake Enneagram inner work while we are engaged in community, we can clearly and compassionately witness that what feels most foreign or difficult to embody can be vastly different by type.[6]

For our healing and transformation, we need community spaces that are not just safe but also *brave*—spaces where others' modeling of authenticity, vulnerability, and courage can continue to inspire our own. In such communities, individuals (including servant-leaders) are earnestly engaged in the work of relating to themselves, each other, and the larger world from a place beyond their habitual and unconscious patterns. Community members actively consider their type when relating to other people both inside and outside the community.

Ultimately, it is not just a community of people that is needed to support individual healing. But as pointed out in Principle 5, our wholeness is by nature communal. Thus, our healing is inseparable from the healing of the community—ultimately the global, interspecies community.[7] Certified Enneagram professional Abi Robins says it so well in *The Conscious Enneagram* where they write extensively about wholeness and (human) community:

> *Wholeness, in the ultimate sense, is not merely about us as individuals but is about what we can experience as we grow in community and connection with one another—learning to hear other voices and perspectives, learning to love all the infinite differences there are between us while understanding that we are intricately connected. This is the kind of wholeness our Enneagram work is really inviting us into. We are finite beings and will always have limitations to what we can see, experience, and understand. That is exactly why we need community. By being in community with another finite being who sees, experiences, and understands things differently than we do, we get to experience more. We can only experience our true wholeness in community. This experience of true wholeness starts in our Conscious Community.[8]*

TIP: The willingness to search for an authentic and compassionate community is an act of courage and faith—especially if we have had hurtful experiences with trusting others in the past. When we allow ourselves to be shaped not only by the support but also by the inevitable challenges of being in community (or any authentic and conscious relationships), we demonstrate commitment to making meaningful progress on our inner journey.[9]

Principle 7: Thou Shalt Not Weaponize the Enneagram

The Enneagram is an incisive instrument. Like a surgeon's knife, the Enneagram can be used to get beneath the skin of our persona and thus to support healing from the inside out. Yet, if used unskillfully, the same instrument can cause further injury. For this reason, I often tell beginning Enneagram students:

I'd rather you not know the Enneagram than apply the Enneagram without compassion.

Even the most well-intentioned among us can find ourselves making flippant remarks or overgeneralizing based on our knowledge of the Enneagram. It can be helpful to consider a few ground rules to help us steer clear of unintentional harm while wielding this powerful tool.

First, let us commit to not using the Enneagram to put others in a box. In the heat of a quarrel with another, for instance, even the best of us might find ourselves wanting to use the Enneagram to defend our own stance and preserve our own sense of self by putting the other person into a category that denies their human complexity: "It's because you're a Two!" we might say. Or, conspiring with coworkers against a boss, we make sweeping statements, such as "All Eights are tyrants!"

When we find ourselves in attack mode, we can try to reframe these limiting characterizations into compassionate perspectives—and then hold those higher perspectives in our own hearts. For example, we might consider:

If I think it's because my sibling leads with Type 2, then it's much harder for him to say "No" to mom's request. How might I support my sibling in this?

Or

If our boss is an Eight, then it makes sense she struggles with impatience. How might we be more assertive, stand our ground, and speak directly to her about how we need more time here?

In relating to others, it is vital to remind ourselves that Enneagram knowledge is meant to be applied first and foremost to *our own* inner work and awakening. For example, a person who leads with Type 1 might notice where they tend to be hypercritical. Consequently, that individual might make gratitude or praise (see Practice 5) an intentional and concerted practice to offset this tendency. In their prayer time, the One might further pray to see the Light in all people, including in themselves.

As we each journey through the mountains and valleys of our own lives, on certain days we'll get grouchy and might become outright spiteful toward others. Let us do our best to catch ourselves before using the Enneagram as a weapon to exploit, blame, or shame anyone in a misguided effort to demonize what seems to be in our way. Conversely, let us also commit to calling ourselves out when we want to use the Enneagram to justify our own behavior by saying something like: "Hey! I'm just a Seven!" or "What do you expect? I'm an Eight!"

Speaking of type labels, ethically, I believe that no one—not even an Enneagram "expert"—has the right to "type" anyone else. Granted, we might have our own perspective and even very accurate guesses. I deeply believe, however, that we violate another's autonomy and can even engage in a form of gaslighting when we insist that we know someone better than they know themselves and, when we do so, we deny the validity of their direct personal experience. Sure, there is a chance that we are correct and someone else has mistyped themselves, but there is also much hubris in deciding we know for sure what is best for someone and that we need to correct or even bully them into believing things from our own inherently biased perspective. Relatedly, sometimes when we think we know someone's type and they seem to have an experience that does not fit our understanding of that type, we can find ourselves wanting to reject their actual experience as they understand it. Perhaps they come from a different racial and cultural background, and perhaps our Enneagram map needs to be updated and redrawn to account for variations in type based on such differences. It is important to maintain humility even as we, as students and professionals, grow in our Enneagram expertise.

Together, let us steward the gift of the Enneagram and help to promulgate this symbol as an ever-widening circle of all-embracing compassion rather than a scepter of polarizing elitism.

Let us enlist the Enneagram as a means for honoring one another's holiness, rather than pointing out one another's perceived brokenness.

Let our knowledge of Ennea-type—both our own and others'—be a doorway rather than a dead end. Let it be a portal for all of us, opening into our larger wholeness and collective unity.

I live my life in widening circles that reach out across the world.

—Rainer Maria Rilke, Austrian poet

Principle 8: The Map Is Not the Territory

The map is not the territory.

—Alfred Korzybski, mathematician

We often teach that the Enneagram is a map of consciousness, yet it serves us all to remember: the map is not the territory. In other words, the description of the thing is not the thing itself. The model is not reality. The abstraction is not the abstracted.

On September 25, 2023, Middleton Police Department reported that charges had been filed against a DoorDash driver who allegedly followed GPS into a body of water in Middleton, Massachusetts. While I find this story to be funny and sad at the same time, it is a good reminder that as we journey in life, it's nice to have a map for reference, but let's not become so occupied with the map that we do not fully perceive what is right here in front of us—and right under us!

Study the Enneagram map, but don't let focusing on the map obscure your vision. Just because something is not on the map does not mean it doesn't exist in your inner (or outer) space. Employ practices such as Inner Observer (Practice 3) to make sure you are open and receptive to what is happening not only in your outer life but also within the territory of your own consciousness.

Principle 9: It Works If You Work It

You may think about things so much that you get into the state
where you are eating the menu instead of the dinner.

—Alan Watts, *Eastern Wisdom, Modern Life*

The Enneagram tells us the nine basic ways our attention is diverted from being present to reality. Devoting ourselves to inner work, especially amid competing outer demands, is itself a leap of faith as well as an act of love for our highest self—a dedication to truth even when we are exhausted and even when so much of this promised "truth" is still quite mysterious and invisible to us. Those who demand "I have to see it before I believe it" cannot cross this threshold. The realizations come to us through a willingness to step forward in faith and thus to practice faith *as a verb*.

Enneagram inner work is certainly not the only way up the figurative mountaintop of enlightened living. Still, if Enneagram inner work calls you, you know it because it nags at you and won't leave you alone. If this is the case, I encourage you: don't stop at just reading this (or any Enneagram book), but give this a real go by dedicating yourself to the contemplative practices, type-based activations, and reflection questions offered here for you. Again, find community to support you and keep you accountable to your own truth. As they say in twelve-step recovery rooms: "It works if you work it, so work it because you're worth it."

NINE PRACTICES

The spiritual journey is paradoxical. It is both effortful and effortless. Indeed, most of us need to exert *considerable* effort to get out of the gravitational pull of our type-trance before we can get into the more easeful inner space of our soul. At the same time, if we've been on the spiritual journey for a while, we know from experience that we can't "effort" (i.e., bootstrap) our way into awakening. Many of us learn this the hard way. In fact, the more we try to work at it (trying to earn our way into miracles, grace, or transformation), the more those experiences elude us. This is, in my view, because that approach starts from the wrong premise.

The harder we do inner work, the more we realize the truth of Albert Einstein's observation: "No problem can be solved from the same level of consciousness that created it." Our current consciousness cannot elevate ourselves to a higher level of consciousness. That said, we *do* play a pivotal part in our own awakening. Spiritual practice is the part we play. It is not transactional. It doesn't *earn* us transformation. It is, rather, cocreative. By our intention and our practices, we seed the soil for the miracle of renewed life. We don't create this life; we cooperate with it and participate in it. To cite a well-known truism:

Enlightenment is an accident. Meditation makes you accident prone.

Following are nine meditative practices to support you in cultivating receptivity to the happy accident of enlightenment. Be advised that many of these practices have a lengthy history and entire books have been written about them. The following section offers a few notes on each depth-full practice—something you can carry with you on your daily treks through the wilderness of consciousness. My dream is that you will feel inspired to delve more deeply into each of these practices using the resources offered both here and in Appendix B.

Don't try to be a spiritual superstar and apply all of these practices in one day. In fact, it would be ideal if you just selected one to three at a time as your core practices. Trust your inner guidance (perhaps with support from a spiritual mentor) when it comes to which ones are best suited to you. I imagine that something will stir in you when you recognize which practices are meant for you at this moment in your life. It is often a strong reaction either toward or against the practice. Consider that this may indicate that there is a gift in that particular practice for you.

Some of these practices you will live with for just a few days. Others, I hope, will become daily companions for weeks or months. Yet others may be touchstones that you carry in your pocket for the rest of your life to nourish your everyday alchemy.

Practice 1: Centering Prayer—"Die Before You Die"

The secret to life is "to die before you die."

—Eckhart Tolle, *The Power of Now*

Many of the world's spiritual and religious traditions have a teaching around the need to "die before we die." This is not a literal but a symbolic death. As St. Paul said, "I die daily."

Centering Prayer helps us to "die" to our egoic identities and be transformed by the renewing of our minds—to be reformed in the light of truth.[1] As Cynthia Bourgeault teaches in *Centering Prayer and Inner Awakening*:

> *The practice . . . is like a "mini-death," at least from the perspective of the ego. . . .*
> *We let go of our self-talk, our interior dialogue, our fears, wants, needs, preferences,*
> *daydreams, and fantasies. These all become just "thoughts," and we learn to let them*
> *go. . . . There is a moment when the ego is no longer able to hold us together, and*
> *our identity is cast to the mercy of Being itself. This is the existential experience of*
> *"losing one's life."*[2]

From an Enneagram perspective, this "mini death" helps to free us from the limiting perspective that we are only our Enneagram types so that we might come to experience our full, divine nature as a gift, not only for ourselves but ultimately for the entire world. Although Centering Prayer begins as a kind of "inner sanctuary" that we *go to*, with dedicated practice, it becomes a center of Divine Radiance that we *come from* as we make space for the Infinite to transform our hearts and minds.

Centering Prayer is not about having to be silent or devoid of thought, which is virtually impossible for most of us. It is about being willing to keep emptying, even as thoughts inevitably begin to fill our minds. We simply withdraw our attention from anything that brings it to a focal point and return again and again to our underlying intention to *rest in God*—or, as I prefer to think of it, *rest in Love*. Bourgeault refers to it as "a wordless, trusting opening of self to the divine presence."[3]

The key to this practice is our heartfelt intention rather than our mindful attention. Unlike other methods of meditation, Centering Prayer does not furnish an object for your attention—whether it be a candle, a mantra, your breath, or something else. Notably, we do not approach our prayer time as if the Divine has been absent. To the contrary, as Father Thomas Keating (the founder of the Centering Prayer movement) counsels: "Centering prayer is not a way of turning *on* the presence of God. Rather, it is a way of saying, 'Here I am.'"[4]

In Centering Prayer, even if your attention wanders all over the place, rest assured that your willingness to keep practicing is enough. In Bourgeault's hopeful words: "Ninety percent of the trick in successfully establishing a Centering Prayer practice lies in wanting to do it in the first place."[5] What a relief, yes? The simple fact that you're reading this suggests you are at least open or even wanting to establish a Centering Prayer practice, which means you're 90 percent of the way there. Congratulations!

The following are the basic steps of this devotional practice. Contemplative Outreach, the organization responsible for training commissioned presenters of Centering Prayer, recommends that you practice at least twice a day for twenty minutes each time.[6] (I've found that it's better, though, if you start with five minutes rather than skipping your practice entirely. I also recommend that you try out Centering Prayer for a solid six months before you decide it is not for you.) The spiritual fruits of this practice are not meant to be sought in the meditation time itself; rather, they emerge over time, often as powerful and unexpected gifts of grace in our everyday lives.

Centering Prayer Steps

STEP 1: Sit up straight (or lie down if you need to).

Keep an upright spine if possible but let your shoulders drop. You want a physical posture that supports alertness but is relaxed and comfortable at the same time.

STEP 2: Pick a "sacred word" to use as an anchor for your practice.

Keep it simple—one syllable is ideal. In my practice, I have used the same word since 2007: *Peace.* Try not to get bogged down in choosing the right word or in repeatedly changing your word. Those efforts will only distract you from the practice. This word is not supposed to be a focal point; to the contrary, use it like a dry eraser. When you see thoughts appear, use the word to clear your mind. The word is a reminder of your intention to self-empty and rest in Love. Also, if you find yourself getting caught up in the meaning of the word, don't give up! Try visualizing a sacred image, such as a candle or a tree, instead. After you have used the word or image to empty your mind, let it go.

STEP 3: Silently, with eyes closed (or open but with gaze lowered if you tend to fall asleep while practicing), recall your sacred word or image to begin your prayer.

As you notice your attention focusing on any thoughts, senses, or feelings, try your best not to judge or chastise yourself. Simply and gently return to your sacred symbol. Do this however many times you notice your attention narrowing to a focal point.

STEP 4: When your prayer period is over, try not to jump into action or speech.

Do your best to transition slowly from your prayer practice to your active life.

> *Your own subjective experience of the prayer may be that nothing happened—except for the more-or-less continuous motion of letting go of thoughts. But in the depths of your being, in fact, plenty has been going on, and things are quietly but firmly being rearranged. That interior rearrangement—or to give it its rightful name, that interior awakening—is the real business of Centering Prayer.*
>
> —Cynthia Bourgeault, *Centering Prayer and Inner Awakening*

Practice 2: Welcoming Prayer—"Come as You Are"

This being human is a guest house. Every morning is a new arrival.
A joy, a depression, a meanness, some momentary awareness comes
as an unexpected visitor. . . . Welcome and entertain them all.

—Rumi, Excerpted from "The Guest House"

Many of us hide from God in prayer. The reason for this is the ways we've
internalized our reading about prayer. We can find ourselves trying to be
quiet, reverent, centered when we haven't acknowledged that as we enter
into the posture of prayer we are, in fact, none of what we are trying to
be. We might in fact be angry, excited, disappointed, tender, or hurt at the
time we choose to pray. We are invited by God to come as we are.

—Barbara Metz and John Burchill, *The Enneagram and Prayer*

Welcoming Prayer is a practice of accepting ourselves exactly as we are in any given moment, rather than judging or analyzing ourselves based on how we think we should be or feel.[7] An ideal practice for beginning or ending one's day, it is also particularly useful to apply this practice whenever triggering emotions arise. In doing so, rather than reject our experience, we embrace it. Welcoming Prayer is a gesture of radical acceptance. It is not about welcoming the triggering conditions or circumstances, such as a medical diagnosis, job loss, or death of a loved one. Rather it is about welcoming the inner experience that arises in us.[8] When we are willing to welcome our experience, we find that Divine Love, indwelling in us, transforms and renews us. Cynthia Bourgeault writes "[Welcoming Prayer is] Centering Prayer's powerful companion piece for turning daily life into a virtually limitless field for inner awakening."[9]

Welcoming Prayer Steps

STEP 1: Identify and sink into the feeling as a sensation in your body.

When the first indications of an emotion or physical upset arise, locate them, and focus on the felt sensation in the body. Where in the body is the emotion felt? Don't judge it. Don't analyze it. Don't try to determine why it is there. Any of those mental acts will only repress your actual experience of it, which prevents it from moving through you. Best you can, just let the sensation be there and sink into it.

STEP 2: Welcome in the presence of Spirit.

From a Unity faith perspective, Spirit is never absent, so technically the invitation here is to welcome the awareness of Spirit (by whatever name you prefer to call your Higher Power). Then, whatever the sensation is, continue to welcome it gently, saying to yourself, *Welcome, pain,* or *Welcome, frustration.* (Remember that it is the sensation that is being welcomed, not the situation that brought it on.) By doing this, you are cultivating an inner hospitality that affirms that everything in us belongs and is welcome. When we welcome our feelings in this way, we limit their power to fuel our Ennea-type's passions and fixations. Don't rush through this step. In fact, repeat steps 1 and 2 until you can honestly and openly welcome your experience.

STEP 3: Surrender.

Finally, surrender—as an inner attitude rather than as an outer practice. This is not about capitulating or passively acquiescing to situations that are in fact intolerable. As Bourgeault puts it,

> *Anything done in a state of interior bracing will throw you immediately into your small self, with its familiar repertoire of defense mechanisms. Surrender understood as an interior act will place you in alignment with magnetic center, the seat of your inner observer, through which Divine Being can flow to you. Once you are in right alignment, you can decide what you are going to do in the outer world. Sometimes this is acquiescence, sometimes it is a spirited fight. But whichever way, you will be doing it from consciousness, not reactivity.*[10]

Surrender requires us to leave behind our personal agenda to experience the peace and bliss of knowing our oneness with the Divine. In this step, you need not rush to let go. Rather, stay with the physical sensation, alternating between observing and welcoming. Then gently release the need to fix anything, to attach stories to the feeling, and wait until the emotional spike has passed. Do not become attached to a happy outcome of this prayer. Just do your part by surrendering. The spontaneous dissipation of the emotion will naturally make space for heart-centered awareness—the foundation for skillful right action rather than unconscious reactivity based on the compulsions of our type. Finally, repeat the following prayer silently or out loud:

I release the need for power and control over this feeling.
I release the need for approval and esteem around this feeling.
I release the need for safety and security around this feeling.
I release the need to change anything about this feeling.
I release the need to change anything about myself.
And so it is. Amen.

Practice 3: Inner Observer—"Turning the Subject into the Object"

The immediate goal is to recognize the inner patterns that drive
your outer behavior. These patterns vary according to the type of
person you are and can be internally witnessed by a faculty
of spiritual awareness commonly called the Inner Observer.

—Helen Palmer, cofounder of The Narrative Enneagram

Self-observation brings man to the realization of the necessity
of self-change. And in observing himself a man notices that
self-observation itself brings about certain changes in his inner
processes. He begins to understand that self-observation is
an instrument of self-change, a means of awakening.

—Gurdjieff

Many of us come to our soul journeys with a decent amount of self-reflection (and often hours of paid therapy or coaching). We might have discovered *why* we do something, but when we try to change our thinking or behavior, we find that we can't. When thrust into a new situation, we lapse into habitual and not always helpful ways.

It is important to distinguish here between self-reflection and self-observation. *Self-reflection* happens after our initial reaction to an event (sometimes seconds, sometimes years afterward). By that time, we have already acted, skillfully or not. We reflect on being at the mercy of our quickest and thus most reactive patterns and have no power to choose differently; the past cannot be remade. *Self-observation*, on the other hand, occurs in the present moment. We are aware of our reaction *as* it is happening.

Variations of the Inner Observer practice appear in all wisdom traditions. The practice set forth here is one I first learned from now-retired master Enneagram teacher Helen Palmer back in 2006 at a The Narrative Enneagram Certification training in Northern California. The practice consists of focusing your attention inwardly and becoming aware of whatever objects of attention arise. Notably, unlike Centering Prayer (Practice 1), which is a practice of releasing our focus of attention, the Inner Observer practice is a practice of *focusing* our attention.

We can exercise our Inner Observer at any time, but it is best to start on occasions when we're not emotionally triggered or in a physically precarious situation (like skydiving). We can practice self-observation while waiting in line at the grocery store or doing chores around the house. This way, we can gradually and safely develop our Inner Observer as a mental muscle.

When we first try to focus our attention on our own thinking, we might be surprised by how difficult it is. Like a person sitting at an outdoor café watching pedestrians and cyclists go by, instead of just observing what is happening, we might start creating a narrative—often filled with judgments—*about* what is happening. This is common and normal. When we realize that we're getting into thoughts about our thoughts, we can simply step back and become the observer of the inner storyteller, judge, or critic.

As we continue to observe our thoughts, feelings, and sensations, we find that our own preoccupations—which are typically derived from our Ennea-type's core passion and fixation—begin to feel more distant from us.[11] The reason for this is that part of our own awareness remains detached enough to watch the flow of thoughts go by. At first, when we are having a thought, feeling, or sensation, we tend to identify with it. We don't generally think, "This angry feeling is happening." Rather, we think, "I am feeling angry" or even "I *am* angry." The more we learn to observe our inner world without judgment or trying to change anything, the more radically and quickly change seems to happen. We begin to recognize that our experiences are phenomena— just like the weather or the outfit we chose to wear today—some things we have control over and some we don't, but none of it is permanent and none of it is *us*. The paradox and gift of the Inner Observer practice is that whatever is being observed automatically transforms without our personal efforts to change it. As soon as we observe something happening within us, the subject ("I") becomes the object ("it"). Over time, we recognize that who (or what) we are is *not* this or that thought, feeling, or the like. This is a spiritual path of negation. Rather than lock down who we are to a pattern of attitudes, beliefs, or experiences, this practice helps us know: *I am not that.* Instead, *I am the awareness able to experience and react in that way—as well as in a multitude of other ways. I am not defined or limited by my type. I am awareness itself. I am free.*

Practice 4: Grounding Practice—"Where Are My Feet?"

*It is only by grounding our awareness in the living sensation of
our bodies that the "I Am," our real presence, can awaken.*

—Gurdjieff

The mind can dwell in the past or the future, but the body inhabits only the present moment. Focusing on the physical (i.e., felt sense) of your body can support you in grounding your awareness in the present moment, which is a prerequisite for authentic self-awareness and inner and outer work. After all, how do you know what is truly here if your attention is not fully here?

"Where are my feet?"

One very easy, quick, and highly accessible way of using your felt-sense lens of perception to arrive in the present moment is to ask yourself this question: *Where are my feet?* Simply noticing your feet, which is *not* the same as analyzing or judging what you are noticing, can serve as a cornerstone of awakening. This inquiry alone, with eyes open or closed, can take you out of reverie or anxious thinking and ground you in the here and now.

If you wish to deepen your practice and further cultivate your capacity for somatic intelligence, after sensing your feet on the ground you might shift attention to your breath. Closing your eyes can be helpful if you struggle to keep your attention inside of yourself but is not necessary. Also, note that this exercise is not about trying to *change* your breathing—or anything else. Rather, it is simply about bringing compassionate curiosity to what is *already* happening within you. Typically, when we shine the light of awareness on any area of our physical or energetic bodies, a shift happens spontaneously. However, this is not about trying to make anything happen. It is simply about being in connection with what is already occurring.

Notice the breath and the ways it flows within your body. Then become aware of the weight of your body and how it is being held by the chair or floor beneath you. Sense how the earth beneath you is supporting you. You might conclude this practice by imagining the energy of your spine and of your feet all rooting into the ground beneath you, stabilizing you.

This helps you to realize that you are here and the moment is now. See if you can move about the rest of your day or evening from this more centered state and when you catch yourself mentally, emotionally, or physically off balance, simply ask yourself: *Where are my feet?* Then pause to take note: Here they are—and *here I am.*

Practice 5: Gratitude—"A Causative Energy"

Abundance is not something we acquire. It is something we tune into.

—Wayne Dyer, author of *The Power of Intention*

In *The Language of Letting Go*, one of America's most renowned addiction and recovery self-help authors Melody Beattie writes: "Gratitude unlocks the fullness of life. It turns what we have into enough, and more. It turns denial into acceptance, chaos to order, confusion to clarity. It can turn a meal into a feast, a house into a home, a stranger into a friend."[12] Centuries before her, Christian mystic Meister Eckhart counseled, "If the only prayer you ever say in your entire life is thank you, it will be enough." Before him, the ancient Roman philosopher Cicero taught that "Gratitude is not only the greatest of the virtues, but the parent of all of the others."

In Unity, we teach that gratitude is a powerful causative energy not a reactive emotion. When we practice gratitude as an intentional practice, we align our mind with the Divine Mind, allowing us to experience ourselves as cocreative participants in life's eternal and abundant flow. Gratitude is different from positively reframing situations, which is a common default among certain Ennea-types—especially the "positive outlook" types (Types 2, 7, and 9). While seeing the positives of a situation is a helpful step in coping with life's difficulties, it is important to guard against gratitude practice becoming a "spiritual bypass."[13] Gratitude as a spiritual practice is not about avoiding painful situations or repressing any negative feelings. Rather, it is about recognizing that as we encounter even the most trying of circumstances, we can be like the biblical Jacob, who wrestled with the angel, enduring until he received a blessing (Genesis 32–33).

In practicing gratitude, we express our appreciation for everything and everyone we encounter—not just for the "happy" experiences. When it comes to our biggest life challenges, like Jacob, we meet them head on with faith and the *expectation* of blessing—even though, through our personality's limited lens, we cannot yet see how this might be so.

Not only does gratitude practice help us realize the abundance of good already here and available to us, as we embody a sense of prosperity, we move beyond worrying about whether we personally have (or are) enough and begin to live from a state of abundance. A key indicator of our gratitude-inspired prosperity mindset is not the amount or quality of things (not even the relationships) we possess; rather, the testament to true wealth is a spirit of generosity. We are wisely and compassionately generous not because someone has told us we "should" give. Instead, we give from our state of overflow. We give because we know we are one with the infinite wellspring of life. When we live from a place of gratitude, we express Divine Abundance. We are naturally generous because we know we lack nothing we truly need to live our highest purpose in this life. To the extent we save up money or other resources, we do so not out of fear but from a place nourished by Spirit—a place of wisdom and of faith—preparing not against potential disaster but instead preparing *for* opportunities to continue to express our highest selves. Lakota author and activist Doug Good Feather says, "Gratitude and generosity are similar virtues, but they differ in that gratitude is an internal characteristic and generosity is our external expression of our sense of gratitude. Basically, gratitude is how we feel, and generosity is how we express that feeling out in the world."[14]

In a state of grateful generosity:

- Ones experience rest in the divine perfection of the moment and inspire acceptance and serenity in all, through all.

- Twos harvest a cornucopia of love and humbly give from what they first allow themselves to receive.

- Threes experience their pearl-like being and mirror the exquisite truth in others in a way that draws their unique presence and purpose forth.

- Fours take to heart the sweetness of joy as well as of sorrow and creatively bring to life the full spectrum of our shared humanity.

- Fives sense their connection to a boundless and interconnected energy field and give freely of their compassionate wisdom.

- Sixes see through eyes of faith and lend an excess of encouragement and fortitude to every situation they encounter.

- Sevens are fully sated within the here and now and share the joy of contentment with others.

- Eights become more fiercely tender with the world and offer the gift of their child-like awe and wonder.

- Nines embrace all points of view and generously contribute their unique voice and grounded vitality.

Practice 6: Mystical Awe—"Be Astonished"

Spiritual practice should not be confused with grim duty.
It is the laughter of the Dalai Lama and the wonder born with every child.

—Jack Kornfield, *A Lamp in the Darkness*

This past weekend, we had to put down our sixteen-year-old golden retriever, Effie. I was struck by how, amid our tears and pain, also within me I felt a sense of beauty and profundity—indeed, of awe—in those last moments as I peered into this being's eyes and poured words of love over her as she gazed steadily back at my partner and his mom and me (her "pack") and took her final breath. As an Enneagram consultant for an innovative program for caregivers of individuals with dementia, I have been blessed to discover how awe is a proven resource that can be called upon during one's most challenging times—to support healing during seasons of burnout, anxiety, or intense grief.

Awe is not reserved for the beginnings or endings of life, however.[15] Many of us have experienced spontaneous awe when confronted with exceptional beauty, vastness, or goodness. In a seminal book on the transformational power of awe, psychology researcher Dacher Keltner defines awe as "the feeling of being in the presence of something vast that transcends your current understanding of the world."[16]

While awe can certainly happen at any time, according to Keltner's studies, we are most likely to experience awe or wonder when experiencing the following "8 wonders of life": moral beauty, collective effervescence, nature, music, visual design, spirituality and religion, birth and death, and epiphany.[17] Notably, the list does *not* include binge watching television shows, playing countless hours of computer or smartphone games, watching endless hours of fear-inducing news, and so forth—certainly not the way our modern society would encourage us to spend our time.

When we experience awe, our eyes literally, yet also figuratively, widen and become more childlike. From a contemplative Enneagram perspective then, awe serves as a spiritual antidote to the Ennea-type's poisoning of our moments with its "same-old, same-old" attitude. Awe and wonder free us from our type-based habits of thinking, feeling, and behaving, lift us over the threshold of our limited, default frameworks, and invite us to gaze and gape and "ooh" and "ahh" at a larger horizon of existence.

Awe also inspires awe. Keltner writes:

You might have thought that when we more often experience awe in the wonders of life, those wonders lose their power. This is known as the law of hedonic adaptation, that certain pleasures—consumer purchases, drinking a savory beer, or eating chocolate, for example—diminish with their increased occurrence. Not so with awe. The more we practice awe, the richer it gets.[18]

The cultivation of awe is perhaps as simple as remembering to introduce activities that tend to inspire a sense of awe into our contemporary lives. Perhaps you might read inspirational stories of kindness and overcoming obstacles. You might choose to take a walk outside, looking around as if you are seeing everything for the first time. You might listen to music—or even join a choir or participate in a chanting group, such as Kirtan or Taizé. If you tend to be visual, you might visit a local art museum or go on an architectural tour. You might volunteer to hold babies, walk shelter dogs, or even serve as a hospice volunteer. These are just a few examples of how you might infuse your everyday life with opportunities for awe.

Not all of us can readily get away to visit the Grand Canyon or chant with Tibetan monks. Especially in times that are challenging or when darkness can appear to overwhelm us, it is helpful to remember that awe is accessible to those who pay attention and who cultivate a kind of "beginner's mind" toward what is familiar. When we pay attention, the simplest things can call to us: the way sunlight filters through the trees, the elegance of a hawk soaring in the sky, the changing faces of the moon, the way each flower opens, a special poem, or our cat's purr.

In her book, *This Here Flesh: Spirituality, Liberation, and the Stories That Make Us*, Cole Arthur Riley observes, "Awe is an exercise, both a doing and a being. It is a spiritual muscle of our humanity that we can only keep from atrophying if we exercise it habitually."[19] Indeed, like gratitude (see Practice 5), awe is a *practice* of paying attention and not taking anything for granted. Noticing keeps us attuned to the pulse of life and offers us a perspective that Rabbi Abraham Joshua Heschel called "radical amazement." Different from a gratitude practice, however, our main "exercise" in this practice is twofold: first, the active "doing" of dedicating attentive time and space, and also the receptive "being" that allows us to be literally and wondrously awestruck.

Practice 7: Namasté—"Beholding the Divinity in All"

The way you alchemize a soulless world into a sacred world is by treating everyone as if they are sacred until the sacred in them remembers.

—Rivka Grace Savitri, Kripalu yoga teacher

In the United States, yoga classes have helped to popularize the *anjali mudra* (AHN-jah-lee MOO-dra), a sacred hand position originating in India. This contemplative posture involves placing our palms together in front of our hearts to signify beholding the Divine in ourselves and the person before us—a deportment that physically mirrors what Christians might call "prayer hands" and that countless wisdom traditions around the world view as an act of reverence.

I first learned the anjali mudra practice in my Unity community concurrent with learning Unity's Truth principle: that God is imminent as well as transcendent—that is to say, *within* me as well as all around me. Having grown up fearing that I was inherently bad and defective (but also somewhat skeptical that this was *really* true—of myself or anyone else), I readily took to Unity's teaching that we are born not in "original sin" but in "original blessing" and that the Divine expresses in all, through all, and *as* all. Since 2005, I have kept the following words posted by the front door in every place I've lived:

> *When you meet anyone, remember it is a holy encounter. As you see them you will see yourself. As you treat them you will treat yourself. As you think of them you will think of yourself. Never forget this, for in them you will find yourself or lose yourself. (A Course in Miracles)*

Beholding the holiness of all life is a purifying, grounding, and generative practice that helps us see beyond our apparent flaws and grounds us in the fundamental truth of our divine wholeness and holiness. The anjali mudra is generally accompanied by the salutation *namasté*. Namasté is a Sanskrit word often translated as "I bow to the divinity within you from the divinity within me."[20] This salutation is a practice of seeing the Divine within all of creation and can be offered equally to all of existence—not just to people but in homage to the sacred in every creature and every mountain, ocean, or tree. We practice this at every Evolving Enneagram gathering and after each person shares in our contemplative Enneagram groups.

While we can certainly hold the sacred prayer intention without employing the anjali mudra, this yogic posture can help us to "seal" and embody the intention. In fact, the term *anjali* means "offering," and the term *mudra* means "seal."[21] There is something about embodying our prayers with a physical gesture that helps bring our spiritual intention into the material world.

To practice this prayer posture, lengthen your spine out of your pelvis and extend the back of your neck by dropping your chin slightly in. With open palms, slowly draw your hands together at the center of your chest as if to gather all your resources into your heart. When done properly, Sri Tirumalai Krishnamacharya, often considered to be the father of modern yoga, teaches, "the palms are not flat against each other; the knuckles at the base of the fingers are bent a little, creating space between the palms and fingers of the two hands resembling a flower yet to open, symbolizing the opening of our hearts."[22]

Repeat that movement several times, contemplating the integration of wholeness through the bringing together of opposites—the right and left side of yourself, the masculine and the feminine, the sky and the earth, logic and intuition, strength and tenderness, and so forth—into wholeness. As yoga teacher Shiva Rea describes it:

> *As you bring your hands together at your center, you are literally connecting the right and left hemispheres of your brain. This is the yogic process of unification, the yoking of our active and receptive natures. In the yogic view of the body, the energetic or spiritual heart is visualized as a lotus at the center of the chest. Anjali mudra nourishes this lotus heart with awareness, gently encouraging it to open as water and light [to] a flower.*[23]

For a deepened experience, you can sense how potent the placement of your hands at your heart can be by experimenting with shifting your hands to one side or the other and pausing there for a moment. Do you feel an imbalance? Now shift your palms back to center and notice how you feel. Only if your flexibility will allow it, gently touch your thumbs into your sternum as if you were ringing the bell to open the door to your heart.[24] Pull back your shoulders to spread your chest open. Feel the space under your armpits as you align your elbows with your wrists. Take a moment to check in: What initial shifts do you experience—in consciousness or in mood? What changes within you as you receive life from this posture?

Start by engaging this namasté practice by beholding the holiness within yourself and others in those circumstances where it feels easiest. For instance, if it's easy for you to perceive the Divine in nature, practice offering namasté to the natural world and it will help you feel held by the world in the same sacred light. Then direct it toward environments or people where it feels more difficult. You might practice it, for instance, toward people with Ennea-types that trigger you the most. You'll find that this prayer helps cultivate an awareness of divinity in both directions. As a final note, the spirit of namasté can be used in any circumstance (with or without the actual physical gesture or spoken word), and you may find it makes the previous practices of awe and gratitude easier for you, as well!

Practice 8: Journaling—"The Still, Small Voice"

> *Journal writing, when it becomes a ritual for transformation,*
> *is not only life-changing but life-expanding.*

—Jennifer Williamson, American attorney and politician

> *Successful journals break the deadlock of introspective obsession.*

—Alexandra Johnson, *Leaving a Trace*

Journaling as a spiritual practice involves contemplating life from our spiritual center. We approach writing not so much from the stance of telling but of listening. Natalie Goldberg, who is known for bringing writing into a form of Zen meditation practice, says,

> *Writing ... is 90 percent listening. You listen so deeply to the space around you that it fills you, and when you write, it pours out of you. ... Listen to the past, future, and present right where you are. Listen with your whole body, not only with your ears, but with your hands, your face, and the back of your neck. Listening is receptivity.*[25]

Set aside ten to fifteen minutes each day to journal from this place of sacred listening. Setting a timer, write without stopping your pen or censoring your thoughts. You can simply write freeform. However, if you prefer to use prompts, the following are daily journaling prompts that have been helpful to those I mentor—especially those who struggle to know what they personally and authentically feel, think, or need.

Daily Journaling Prompts

Each day, journal each of the following three times—in the morning, at the end of the workday, and before bed:

- *"I feel* [fill in the blank]*."*
- *"I think* [fill in the blank]*."*
- *"I need/want* [fill in the blank]*."*

Whether you are using these prompts, other prompts, or none at all, when you journal as a spiritual practice, write as if no one else will ever read your writing but you. You can later choose to share your writing with others. However, it is important that you write *as if* others will not see it so your inner world has complete safety to show up. Write even if you think you are just rambling or repeating yourself or uttering nonsense. Remember:

> Sometimes our minds need to dump information onto paper so we can become clear-headed. Sometimes our hearts need to emote onto the page so that we can uncover the deeper feelings that underlie our initial, more surface reactions.

Indeed, occasionally, silent meditation simply refuses to happen *because* something deep within us has something important to say. So instead of trying to shut off our minds, we can deliberately trace our mental thought-trail on paper and see where it leads us. At the end of our journaling journey, we might find a place of perfect silence and stillness, or even hear the "still, small voice" (1 Kings 19:12) of Spirit. As Goldberg says,

> *we were taught in [Zen] meditation to continually cut through our wandering, obsessive thoughts and come back to the breath. I understood the importance of this, how we learn to let go . . . but I also noticed I had a fascination with those thoughts . . . what if I actually followed my thoughts, went out into the tangle, saw where they led, used writing as another way to eventually let go?*[26]

Journaling can empty us in a way that renders us more hospitable to the light of Truth.

Practice 9: Affirmative Prayer—"And So It Is"

Prayer is more than supplication. It is an affirmation of Truth that eternally exists, but which has not yet come into consciousness. It comes into consciousness not by supplication but by affirmation.

—Charles Fillmore, Unity cofounder

This is our method of prayer: acknowledging our oneness with God, claiming the ability that this gives, and expecting to have the things needed and conducive to spiritual progress.

—Myrtle Fillmore, Unity cofounder

In Unity, prayer is affirmative rather than supplicatory. "Affirmative Prayer" is empowering prayer.[27] Affirmations are seen as "a statement of truth we use as an anchor for our mind. Just as we know the sun is always shining behind a cloudy sky, we can know the truth about wholeness, abundance, and harmony, while moving through illness, financial strain, and disharmony."[28]

Through affirmative prayer, we realize the infinite power and omnipresence of Spirit. Through affirmative prayer, we recognize our power to cooperate with the divine ideals of wholeness, abundance, and harmony. We shift the focus of our attention away from our outer circumstances and our erroneous belief in separation. We turn our attention inwardly to realize our divine nature and the reality of our oneness with God. From this state of conscious communion, we claim and declare the Truth beyond our circumstances and realize our capacity to think and act accordingly.

Affirmative Prayer Steps

Following are Unity's basic steps for practicing Affirmative Prayer to support you in coming into alignment with Truth, which lies beyond appearances.[29] The key is not in performing the steps perfectly. The key is in cultivating a sense of peace and wellbeing by being willing to release ideas of lack and limitation and open yourself to the felt experience of faith in immutable divine truths.

STEP 1: Relax.

Receive your breath, drop your shoulders, unfurrow your brow, unclench your jaw, release busy thoughts, and focus your attention within.

STEP 2: Concentrate.

Focus your attention on the ever-present power and presence of Spirit as eternal life, unconditional love, boundless wisdom, and all-encompassing good. It might help to inhale "God is," and exhale "I AM."

STEP 3: Meditate.

Drop into silence and stillness to make space for an experience of the Divine in and as you, so that you know you share as your essence all the attributes of God—love, strength, wisdom, and so forth.

STEP 4: Realize.

Arrive at the felt realization of these spiritual truths not merely as ideas but as an experience in your own consciousness. Through this, you come to know that all is well, regardless of outer circumstances. Spirit is already fully present here and now.

STEP 5: Give thanks.

You are not thanking an entity "out there." This is about taking a moment to allow a spontaneous sense of appreciation to arise based on your faith-filled knowing that all is already well and everything you need to live your highest life is already here.

In practicing Affirmative Prayer, remember that we are not trying to make something true that is not true. We are simply releasing our misplaced faith in thoughts of lack and limitation as we proclaim the spiritual Truth (albeit invisible or as yet unmanifested) that underlies it. Because, through our practice of faith, we know the good is already maximally here, we give thanks even before we take action toward worldly outcomes. This is why we always end affirmative prayers with thanksgiving and proclaim: And so it *is*. Amen.

NINE PRAYERS

Prayer does not change God, but it changes [the one] who prays.

—Soren Kierkegaard, Danish theologian and philosopher

The following nine prayers are tailored to each of the nine Ennea-types. However, you might find it helpful to review them all. Further, while it is not essential, practicing Affirmative Prayer (Practice 9) can help prepare your consciousness to fully receive these prayers as nourishment for your soul.

Prayer for Type 1: Accepting What Is

I release my role as judge and jury.
I release my conviction that my way is the only right way
and that my truth is the ultimate truth.

I relax my attention on inner and outer error.
I relax my grip on the need for inner and outer order.

When my worldly eyes simply cannot see it,
I invite my inner eye of faith to allow me to feel it.
I open my heart to be cleared of unforgiveness.
I open my heart to experience the perfection of this moment.

There is beauty and wholeness in this glorious creation
both within me and all around me.

I welcome forgiveness into my heart.
I welcome wisdom into my heart.
I welcome compassion into my heart.
I welcome acceptance into my heart.

Not as an act of resignation
but in the spirit of faith,
I stand down.

Setting aside my need to be right,
I approach the steady altar of my faith.
I kneel before a higher truth,
I open my arms wide,
I accept the invisible Holiness in All That Is.
Right here and right now
I rest on holy ground.

And so it is. Amen.

Prayer for Type 2: Honoring My Needs

Divine Love within me,
embrace my deepest needs,
nurture my greatest joys, and
nudge me to care not only for others,
but also, *for myself.*

I need not beg for love
I need not cajole another
to better honor me.

I simply release any shame over having needs;
any sense of neediness, desperation;
any possessiveness of loved ones;
and my limiting, self-fulfilling belief
that no one *willingly* takes care of me.

I willingly ask for help,
and I receive loving help
from expected and unexpected sources—
from the Divine indwelling and
from others who share this precious Earth.

Among all life, I feel beloved and connected.
From all of life, I receive willingly.
And I let my receiving open and humble me.

Right here and right now,
I willingly honor the sacred love already within me.
I recognize that I have precious and valid hopes and desires
all worthy of reverence, worthy of respect,
all worthy of my own sacred devotion.

And so it is. Amen.

Prayer for Type 3: Knowing My Worth

I release my inner taskmaster.
I release image crafting.
I release continually compartmentalizing my feelings
just to get more done
just to feel more seen.

I let go of pretenses
of trying to prove
how I am better than others
only inasmuch as I feel less than worthy
to simply and authentically
be me.

Today, I offer my inner life
a truce
I offer my own heart
a sanctuary
of faith and hope—
a place where I am fully seen, held, and loved
by me.

I willingly shift from seeing things
in terms of "I"
and sense into how life changes
as I feel into the space
of "us" and "we."

I move from needing to stand higher and apart
to needing only to share together and within
the wholeness and unity of life.

Guide me, sweet Spirit,
in the ways of slow walkers.

Lend me the courage
to face my shame
to speak my truth

to make time to go beyond how I seem
(even to myself)
to enter into the realization of who I
authentically am.

The Truth unmasked is not the
nothingness
or emptiness I fear.
Or the hollowness I've long felt.

Inside,
I'm full of good. I'm full of God.
I *am* whole and worthy
not only in the eyes of the Divine,
but beneath my own sweet, tender gaze.

In the spirit of truth, Amen.

Prayer for Type 4: My Uniqueness Belongs

Today, I embrace the simplicity of everyday life.

As I courageously release my pining for what has been and
faithfully surrender fantasies about what might be,
I come to peace and equanimity in the present moment.

Knowing that my beauty is innate
and my specialness is divinely given,
I release the need for blame or shame—
whether toward myself or another—
I release the compulsion to long for the past
and commit to no longer abandoning myself in the here and now.

I belong here and now without needing to conform.
I recognize I am special in this moment without needing to specially stand apart.

Here I am, Universe!
Here I am, Beloved Heart.

Here and now, nothing is missing.
Here and now, everything is present
because, finally, I *am* present.

Here I am, Great Spirit—
free of the compulsion to dramatize my life experience,
free of the need to compare my life to others,
I embrace myself as the unique and beautiful expression of the Infinite
that I already AM.

And so I authentically am. Amen.

Prayer for Type 5: Living the Mystery

I rest my hands on my lap
open my palms toward the sky
lower my head toward my heart
and willingly bow to the Great Mystery of life.

I surrender small-minded, petty thoughts
that want to compartmentalize and box all of life
into manageable subjects of observation and study.

I open my awareness to eternal wisdom
which cannot be grasped by intellect alone
and willingly experience embodied knowing.

I open my heart to infinite compassion
that I may grieve and forgive past wounds
and thereby retrieve my long-buried hopes and desires.

I open my eyes to spiritual faith
that I may perceive the abundance all around me
and feel the capacity to share from my inner wealth.

Release me
from my tendency to detach and withhold
and from my fear of rejection
that I may engage life with boldness and courage
and feel life's abundance coursing through me.

I am willing to experience anew
how my giving to others
gifts me.

With an open heart,
I experience joy and nourishment
from connecting with others.

With an open mind,
I experience wisdom pouring forth
from the core of my being.

With a receptive body,
I no longer wall or withhold myself
from participating fully in life.

I live and move and have my being
not isolated from but always within
the great cosmic circle
of life.

And so it is. Amen.

Prayer for Type 6: Trusting My Inner Wisdom

Here, now, I claim that
Divine Wisdom and Guidance
are fully present within me.

Within me
is a refuge for trusting myself.
Within me
is a heart of courage.
Within me
is a firm and faithful ground of being.

Within me, I experience a spiritual stronghold—
a sense of surety and security
far greater than any source of security
that any worldly circumstance might offer.

Centered within,
I release fear and mistrust, including mistrust of my own thinking.
I release worry and doubt, freeing myself of my own second guessing.
I release burdening myself with the responsibility of keeping everyone I love safe.
I release the doubt that I do not have what it takes to meet this moment of life.
I release my attention on all that might go wrong.

I open myself to embracing
what is—and what might actually
go—splendidly well and right.

I do not need to have all my ducks in a row.
I need only to check in for guidance for what I need
in the here and now.

Centered within,
I experience peace from whirling or anxious thinking.
I experience much deserved joy and relaxation.
I experience all of life, including myself, as whole and holy.

I stand strong and faithful, with arms open to life's good,
rooted confidently in this present moment
nurtured by this holy ground.

And so it is. Amen.

Prayer for Type 7: I Am Present

I now release spreading myself too thin
trying not to miss out on any one thing
so that I end up missing out on everything
because my attention is scattered.

I now release obsessive planning
and entertaining endless new ideas
that somehow leave me endlessly seeking
yet unfulfilled.

I slow down my pace
to reunite with my heart
and to feel myself being held
in the embrace of the Divine.

Held in this Infinite Love,
I honor all of my emotions,
including the difficult ones like sadness or anger.
I release the fear that negativity will keep me down forever.
I release the need to feel responsible for keeping life upbeat.

I savor life's blessings.
I pay closer attention.
I give myself the gift of noticing
the abundance and radiance that is already here.

With my feet planted on the ground,
I sense how silence is not empty.
As I stay with silence,
I find within it a deep calm.
I sense how stillness is not boring.
As I stay with stillness,
I experience nurturing and deep restoration.

Ahhh! The good I've been searching the world for through each new distraction and exciting adventure has been right here, all along.

For this, I feel profoundly grateful.

And so it is. Amen.

Prayer for Type 8: Courageous Vulnerability

I welcome the gentle spirit of compassion
and allow Divine forgiveness and mercy to flow through me.

As I receive love into my own heart,
I allow myself to feel tenderness for myself and others.
I am willing to see my own childlike innocence and
the innocence in all people.
I allow Divine Mind to reveal to me
a felt and embodied sense of life's unity
beneath our polarizing ideologies and other
outer differences.

I release my role as the judge and jury of all people.
I release seeking vengeance as a means of freeing me from my pain.
I release believing that people are divided into those who are for me and those who
are against me.
I release needing to always be powerful and in control.
I release assuming that more is better.
I release armoring my heart.
I release allowing my pride to ruin my health and relationships
and becoming others' champion but not my own.

I remember and I honor
the parts of me that feel weak, vulnerable, or scared.
I remind myself that as a human being,
I possess legitimate physical limitations and emotional needs,
like everyone else.

As I feel into my own needs,
I treat myself with more gentleness and humanity.
I expose the vulnerable parts of me
to receive long-deserved care and nurturing
both from myself and from others.
I release controlling how that nurturing must happen.

As I look into the mirror
and gaze deeply into my own eyes, I see clearly:
I am a dear, precious, and beloved
child of the Most High.

In my daily life,
I make an intentional place for patience and stillness.
I make room for rest and relaxation.
I yield to that Higher Power and Divine Wisdom—
to this power greater than myself,
consenting to its place in my life,
and believing that this Loving Benevolence
desires my greatest good.

And so it is. Amen.

Prayer for Type 9: My Presence Matters

Holy Love encircles all of me,
shining the light of compassionate awareness
on my authentic feelings, hopes, needs, and desires,
letting me know that I matter
and giving me permission to show up and shine.

Supported by this all-encompassing compassion,
I release my resistance to my inner journey,
I release withdrawing from difficulty or discomfort,
I release falling asleep to my own needs, dreams, and perspectives.

I commit to waking up more fully to my life and
and engaging wholeheartedly in the world.
I commit to discerning and giving voice to
my personal dreams and perspectives
and my own unique life expression.

I willingly shine a light on my own anger.
I make space for this inner volcano:
I listen to its roar or rumble,
I make space for its heated presence,
I willingly hear it out,
I allow this inner fire to guide me in
knowing more of my own truth.

Here, now, and always,
Unconditional Love offers me a key
and holds open this door
inviting me to remember myself,
allowing me to go deep within
and explore the full range of my feelings and desires.
Allowing me to be more honest and authentic
in all of my relationships.

Help me to release judgment against
taking up space

so I can take my rightful place
in the unity of all life.
And to remember that
true harmony and unity embrace
not only all other people and creatures
but also all parts of me—
the dark as well as the light.

In the spirit of peace, love, and unity,
Amen.

PART II

Forty Activations

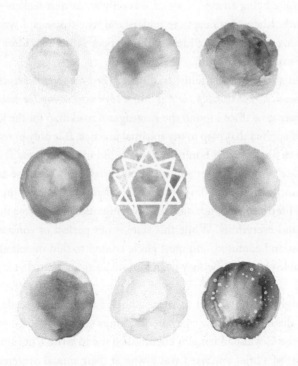

The spiritual quest is a journey without distance. You travel from where
you are right now to where you have always been. From ignorance
to recognition, for all you do is see for the first time what you have
always been looking at. Whoever heard of a path that brings you to
yourself or a method that makes you what you have always been?
Spirituality, after all, is only a matter of becoming what you really are.

—Anthony de Mello, Indian priest and psychotherapist

Since childhood, I knew I would one day write a book. I wanted my book to help people more clearly know *who* they are and *why* they are here—just as I looked to books to do this very thing for me. Yet the fact is that for the first few decades of my life, despite being an avid reader, I was only an earnest seeker—not actually a finder—of truth. I have since come to understand why this was: I was looking for a sense of meaning and purpose in ideas without appreciating that ideas are but pointers toward an experience of truth.

As is often said in the Buddhist tradition: *When the spiritual teacher points their finger at the moon, do not worship the finger and then miss seeing the moon.* It has been over two decades now since I found the Enneagram road map for the journey toward wholeness and applied that map to my spiritual practice. It is only in recent years that I have started to finally feel at home in myself—and in the universe at large. A world that once felt, at best, indifferent and cold now feels deeply intimate and supportive. Most significantly, I feel more love in my heart than I could have imagined experiencing in this lifetime—love not only for my authentic self but love that pours forth for everyone and everything. While this state is not perfect or constant, even when I falter, get lost and confused, and must circle around to find myself all over again, I sense an invisible ground of Being within me and all around me that is both steadfast and forgiving.

Even though I actively tried to write a book for the past decade, I would find myself sitting distractedly at my computer for hours each week to no productive end. Then, during the Covid pandemic, a client asked me to write Enneagram type affirmations as part of a brief seminar I was giving at their annual conference. The event went well—it came and went in a flash—but what it initiated in me was a tidal wave of creative flow!

I realized I had been striving to write, and all I really needed to do was share what I *already* knew to be helpful from my twenty-plus years of doing inner and outer work with the Enneagram. From that day forward, I spent about four hours a day in a joyful stream of what felt like inspired writing. I wrote one daily reflection, affirmation, or practice for *each* of the nine Ennea-types for over ninety days straight!

As I posted these "invitations" to social media, people kept asking, "Do you have a book of these?" As I explored the invitations with my contemplative Enneagram practice community, I witnessed rich insights, healing, and transformation as individuals reflected on them together in Enneagram-literate, inter-spiritual community.

When Michael Pye of Hampton Roads Publishing reached out to me a year ago to see if I was interested in authoring a book, it felt like divine providence. Of the ninety activations I wrote during my pandemic writing spree, I selected exactly forty to share with you here, adding some instruction and reflection questions to guide you through them. I chose forty because this number is associated with the spiritual journeys of prophets and seekers in ancient texts, including Jesus, Moses, Muhammad, and Buddha. Its themes of ego death and spiritual rebirth resonate with the purpose of this book. Forty, in many spiritual texts, is a number symbolizing not only maturation but also the intention to follow something through to completion.

The following forty activations of your innate potential are here to catalyze and support your journey of conscious awakening. These activations are a medley of daily invitations, affirmations, and reminders. Each activation is focused around one overarching theme and tailored to each Ennea-type. I chose to call them *activations* to reflect the fact that they are, indeed, designed to activate or catalyze your growth.

Although they are intended to point you toward wholeness and oneness, these invitations can also sometimes feel uncomfortable or disquieting to the personality—even as they aspire to ultimately bring comfort and healing to the soul. You'll find that some of the most challenging practices offered herein—perhaps the ones you least want to consider, much less revisit—are echoed throughout multiple activations. This reverberation is deliberate, and in fact essential, to helping you dive beneath the surface of your personality.

Remember that this book is not meant to be consumed in one sitting; rather it is intended to be savored and digested slowly over time—and ideally with fellow soul-journers. Take as long as you need with each activation. Repeat the full cycle of forty as many times as you like. The inner journey tends to be spiral-like, rather than linear, with each inward progression looking eerily like the last. Throughout our lifetime, we are invited to visit the same lessons repeatedly to find how the ideas appear to be the "same" but not really, because *we* have changed—and a new depth of realization and freedom is available to us.

Can these activations really help you wake up more fully to the truth of your being? I heartily believe so, *if* you are willing to take the words off the pages of this book and put them into practice in your daily life.

Are you ready? Welcome to the threshold of a more soulful, authentic, and purposeful existence! May you experience more of your intrinsic wholeness—in unity with yourself, others, and the Infinite! Let's begin.

Life is a full circle, widening until it joins the circle motions of the infinite.

—Anaïs Nin, French-American diarist and essayist

What Is Adorable About You

Your task is not to seek for love, but merely to seek and find
all the barriers within yourself that you have built against it.

—Rumi

Seeking love keeps you from the awareness
that you already have it—that you are it.

—Byron Katie, American author

Too often, we begin new books or journeys with a problem-solving, self-help mindset, asking: How do I fix myself or my life? Certainly, the apparent problems and resulting pain in our lives can be motivating. But what if seeing yourself, others, or perhaps even your whole life as a problem to be fixed furthers a "lack" mentality that ensures you will never arrive?

What would change for you if you were willing to let Divine Love inspire your journey? What might happen if you invited Love to flow through all of you right here and now? This is not about forcing yourself to feel self-love or self-acceptance, which might or might not feel authentic to you at this moment. What if all you need to do is be willing to accept yourself as you are today and to ask Love to show you the rest of the way? Are you willing to see yourself more clearly—to let go of any graven images of not-enough-ness and let Love embrace all of you as you are?

Recently, after my morning's Centering Prayer sit (see Practice 1), I was thinking about some of the beautiful individuals I have worked with these past decades, and I had this thought:

So-and-so has no idea how adorable and lovable they are when they . . .

Thus, this activation was born. We hear far too often about what *appears* to need fixing about ourselves, one another, and our world. Let us instead begin by embracing the beauty that is already fully present within us. Let us launch this journey together by giving ourselves permission to love and accept ourselves as we find ourselves today.

I invite you to consider some of the qualities in yourself that you tend to dismiss, that you overlook, or that make you cringe. Consider giving yourself permission to show up in life more with these parts of yourself. Consider the perspective that these are precious parts of your unique humanity—and they are capable of being adored.

Activation by Type[1]

e1: You have no idea how adorable and lovable you are when

- ᴘ you show your precious idiosyncrasies (which you might call "flaws" or "imperfections").

- ᴘ you admit you were wrong and apologize for it. (We're more likely to feel relieved that you're human than to condemn you for your mistakes!)

e2: You have no idea how adorable and lovable you are when

- ᴘ you say "No," or "No, thank you" (and we can tell you're practicing healthy boundaries for perhaps the first time in your life!).

- ᴘ you speak about your own joys, goals, and creative pursuits (rather than just how you're supporting others').

e3: You have no idea how adorable and lovable you are when

- ᴘ you open up the floodgates and let us be with you while you are messy and weepy.

- ᴘ you are simply enjoying yourself candidly in the moment and don't realize anyone is looking.

e4: You have no idea how adorable and lovable you are when

- ᴘ you are being gentle and kind with yourself.

- ᴘ you smile from an authentically joyful place. (Did you know how easily you can light up a room?)

e5: You have no idea how adorable and lovable you are when

- ᴘ you share your feelings (and not just your thoughts).

- ᴘ you are courageously trying to do something new with which you are not yet well versed (and you let others encourage and support you).

e6: You have no idea how adorable and lovable you are when

- you give yourself permission to relax—to be a bit "irresponsible" even— and let yourself simply enjoy our shared time together.

- you step boldly into the limelight and courageously and compassionately shine light on your truth.

e7: You have no idea how adorable and lovable you are when

- you slow down and become fully present.

- you are sad or broken-hearted and let us be with you amidst it.

e8: You have no idea how adorable and lovable you are when

- you turn inward and are tender with yourself.

- you let yourself receive support (especially emotional support).

e9: You have no idea how adorable and lovable you are when

- you express your truth (especially when it contradicts the view of those you care about).

- you are decisive (even at the risk we won't agree with or like the choice you make).

Reflect: How often do you give yourself permission to show up more fully with parts of yourself you have previously tended to guard, condemn, or hide? Has your perspective on what is "adorable and lovable" about you changed at all? Explain.

No amount of self-improvement can
make up for any lack of self-acceptance.

—Robert Holden, British psychologist and author

DAY 2

Opening to Another Way

*Miracles begin when we consider the
possibility that there might be another way.*

—Marianne Williamson, American author

Our responses to life's ups and downs can become so habitual that we tend to assume our most frequent, speediest reactions are inevitable because it's "just who we are." The transformative power of the Enneagram lies in recognizing that we are so much more than the sum of our conditioned responses. The irony is that the more we begin to accept ourselves as we are, the less attached we become to showing up in a certain way—especially when that way is exhausting and limiting. This capacity to be less defended and to welcome another possibility is the beginning of authentic freedom.

In the following activation, notice whether you tend to respond to challenges in a manner that is predictable according to your Ennea-type, and see if you are willing to try out a new approach. The spiritual adage "It's simple but not easy" applies here. This inner journey is not always easy, but it does get easier over time as we willingly loosen our grip on old habits of the mind and open to new possibilities that lie well beyond our current imaginings.

Begin with your type's activation. Then be open to miracles!

Activation by Type

e1: When you think you've done something bad or wrong, you tend to punish yourself through harsh self-condemnation. Even if only for one day, try radical self-acceptance rather than self-lashing. Then see what happens.

e2: When you feel rejected by someone you care about, you tend to go straight to over-adapting to repair the relationship. Try reaching in before reaching out. If only for one day, extend grace to your own heart first, sending love to all the parts that feel shameful or unlovable. Then see what happens.

e3: When you feel you've failed at something important to you, you'll want to quickly reframe it as a success so you won't have to deal with feelings of shame.

If only for one day, try admitting to yourself where you've fallen short of your goals, while also affirming to yourself that you are worthy anyway. Then see what happens.

e4: When you feel as if you're not able to be true to yourself in relationships, you tend to withdraw into mental fantasies. Try reengaging with others and relating to them based not only on what is real for you, but also what might be real for them. If only for one day, focus on understanding the other person's feelings, needs, and perspectives. Then see what happens.

e5: When you feel woefully incompetent in an area that interests you, you tend to become an "expert" in a field of practice without ever actually practicing it at all. Like a couch athlete, you might readily criticize others' actions while rarely, if ever, joining in the game. So, take that exotic trip. Join Toastmasters. Take up golf. Take violin lessons. If only for one day, take concrete action in an interest you've been researching, even if you are not good at it. Then see what happens.

e6: When something awful happens that you neglected to foresee, you tend to beat yourself up for not planning for that contingency. If only for one day, give yourself a break from believing that any degree of preparedness can completely immunize you or those you love from harm or protect you from all dangers. Try recalling the innumerable times you've responded to immediate threats with extraordinary courage and competency. Then see what happens.

e7: When you don't get what you want, you can be quick to abandon ship and make haste toward all the upcoming new and exciting possibilities. Chances are you have been avoiding feelings of sadness, fear, or loneliness without realizing it. Due to your habit of excessive self-reliance and your lack of trust in nurturing, you can tend to think you either can't handle painful feelings or that you need to feel them by yourself. If only for one day, try letting yourself seek others' support tending to your hurt feelings before running off via escapist thoughts or actions. Try being open-hearted to what feels negative inside. Then see what happens.

e8: When you feel directly threatened, you tend to lash out with fiery rage, later paying for it with uncrossable divides littered with the ashes of bridges you never intended to burn. Try dropping beneath your anger and into your heart to see the tenderness your fierceness is trying to protect. If only for one day, try responding to perceived threats from your vulnerable heart rather than flame-throwing before asking questions. Then see what happens.

e9: When those around you are not doing okay, you tend to bend over backward to reduce tension and keep the peace. The problem with this strategy is that it's often unconscious. You don't even realize you've bottled up your own wants or needs. You might say "Yes" when you don't really mean it. Your anger might explode unexpectedly—and at the least opportune time! As difficult as this can be, try to get clear and honest with yourself about what is really going on in you. If only for one day, find a quiet space, and ask yourself: *What am I needing or feeling right now and how do I gently but firmly express this?* Then see what happens.

Reflect: What challenges, if any, did you face in applying your type's activation? Were you able to catch yourself in your type's habitual reaction? If so, were you able to try the different, kinder approach suggested here for your type? If you were able to apply the alternate approach, what resulted? Did you feel differently about the initial trigger or challenge? Did you come to feel differently about yourself?

> *Miracles occur naturally as expressions of love.*
> *The real miracle is the love that inspires them. In this*
> *sense, everything that comes from love is a miracle.*
>
> —*A Course in Miracles*

Good Question!

*The quality of your life is a direct reflection of the
quality of the questions you are asking yourself.*

—Anthony Robbins, American author and coach

Have you ever had a profound insight simply because someone asked you a very good question? Have you ever been annoyed because someone asked you a question and did not wait for your response?

The following activation is not just about asking yourself the question for your type, it is about giving yourself ample space and time to answer. Journaling the question and your answers might help. As you continue to ask and answer the same question over time, you will begin to arrive at answers that might surprise you as they come from a deeper place within you.

Activation by Type

e1: What is the real reason I am upset?

e2: What have I bartered for love?

e3: How do I hide behind my successes?

e4: Who am I beyond what I feel at this moment?

e5: How does uncertainty enhance my life?

e6: How have leaps of faith brought me unimagined good?

e7: How often do I miss out on the joy of the present moment?

e8: How does my resistance to vulnerability keep me small?

e9: How much energy do I expend to stay unaffected?

Reflect: What new insights did you experience, if any? Did you experience things you already knew intellectually but realized in a fresh or different or deeper way?

Compassionate curiosity about the self does not mean liking everything we find out about ourselves, only that we look at ourselves with the same nonjudgmental acceptance we would wish to accord anyone else who suffered and who needed help.

—Gabor Maté, *When the Body Says No*

DAY 4

Freedom from Your Inner Critic

*I found in my research that the biggest reason people aren't
more self-compassionate is that they are afraid they'll become
self-indulgent. They believe self-criticism is what keeps them
in line. Most people have gotten it wrong because our
culture says being hard on yourself is the way to be.*

—Kristin Neff, American author and researcher

The inner critic is the voice that tends to shame and blame us into acting one way and not another. It might tell us to be strong—*"don't be a wuss," "don't cry."* It might berate us incessantly for an error we made at work. It might call us names like *stupid, idiot,* or *fool.* It might try to shame us into staying in an unhealthy relationship because, it tells us, we're not worthy of a better one. Or it might sabotage our attempts at intimacy because it says we're better on our own anyway. (These are just a few examples.)

The inner critic is *not* a monster, but it can still show up in monstrous ways in its inexpert attempts to protect you from harm. Don't demonize it, but don't let this scared part of you govern your life actions and decisions. Practice observing it with gentle compassion. Notice how it is trying to be helpful but is misguided in its approaches—and how it often keeps you from living more honestly and fully.

The following activation addresses how you might start to compassionately observe your own inner critic, which tends to have various nuances to its voice depending on your Ennea-type.

Activation by Type

e1: Your inner critic wasn't designed to be satisfied. After all, its primary purpose is to find and correct errors. Attempting to fashion your day around trying to please or placate this inner critic is therefore a futile and even self-harming endeavor. Recognizing this is the beginning of greater spiritual freedom.

Ask yourself: *What if I didn't really need the inner critic's observations and advice to show up well? What if I listened to the gentler voice of love in me instead?*

e2: Your inner critic doesn't know what love truly is. It tells you that your ability to meet others' needs is what makes you loved and lovable, when what it really does is cause you to feel resentful and desperately starved of care. Recognizing this is the beginning of greater spiritual freedom.

Ask yourself: *What if I was able to be less dependable in relation to others and more reliable when it comes to showing up for myself? What if that which my inner critic thinks is "selfish" is really just basic self-compassion and self-love?*

e3: Your inner critic thinks you're not a good gauge of your own value. It nudges you to persistently solicit feedback from others. Then if you dare to think you *do* have worth, it coaches you to think bigger and will spout off the endless litany of hurdles it has charted for you to finally prove it. Recognizing that your inner critic's job is to move the goalpost is the beginning of greater spiritual freedom.

Ask yourself: *What if my worth was not found at the finish line but, rather, given at the starting point of my life? What if my only real objective is to be the most authentic me?*

e4: Your inner critic's job is to make sure you never feel like you quite fit in. It acts as if it's making an honest, objective comparison of you with others but has already judged you as being less-than and always falling short. Your inner critic pretends to soothe you with bedtime stories filled with suffering and shame, which haunt your days. Recognizing all this is the beginning of greater spiritual freedom.

Ask yourself: *What if my existence is incomparably magnificent? What if my joy is more authentic than my pain?*

e5: Your inner critic thinks you're better off alone. It is easier to convince your mind of this than to justify it to your heart, so it locks your heart up in the basement and hardly ever checks to see if it's okay. Your inner critic tries not only to keep you feeling separate from others but also from parts of yourself, telling you you're better off this way. Recognizing the ways your inner critic is trying to keep you safe is the beginning of greater spiritual freedom.

Ask yourself: *If I cultivated body and heart awareness as well as intellectual under-standing and if I let all three parts guide me, how differently would I live? Would I engage with the world more often and more fully?*

e6: Your inner critic tells you not to trust anything or anyone completely and then attacks you for being chronically anxious, second-guessing, and afraid. Its mixed messages are a way it keeps you on your toes, which is how it thinks you're best protected from life's imminent, underlying dangers. Recognizing that cultivating inner confusion is part of your inner critic's protective strategy is your gateway to experiencing greater spiritual freedom.

Ask yourself: *What if I let myself trust just one thing fully—and that is my own inner wisdom and judgment?*

e7: Your inner critic gets highly anxious and irritable if you make any choices that might narrow your path or slow you down. Behind its surface annoyance is a deep fear that if you slowed down, then past grief or hurt would catch up to you (and your inner critic's frantic efforts to save you from pain will be for naught). Recognizing this is the beginning of greater spiritual freedom.

Ask yourself: *What if I've been running on empty without realizing it? What if slowing down is ultimately the path to happiness beyond my wildest imagination?*

e8: Your inner critic pushes you to act strongly and boldly in the world but treats you as if you're an emotional weakling inside. It thinks by shaming and hiding your tenderness, it can protect you at all costs from hurt, betrayal, or rejection. It doesn't want to risk letting someone else have influence, much less control over you, lest you end up feeling wounded, or like a victim in some way. Recognizing this is the beginning of greater spiritual freedom.

Ask yourself: *What if even the softest parts of me are stronger than I think? What if they didn't need the inner critic as their guard dog?*

e9: Your inner critic tries to keep you safe by cautioning you to stay unseen and unheard; never expressing strong feelings or opinions or making waves in any way. It tells you that your views do not matter, and your contributions aren't important anyway—so why bother? Your inner critic thinks you're better off believing this story than risking showing up in the world and having your deepest fears of insignificance proven right. Recognizing this self-protective censorship is the beginning of greater spiritual freedom.

Ask yourself: *What if I found that in speaking up more, I do matter—not just to others but to myself? What if, when I show up more fully, my life starts to matter more to me?*

Reflect: What happens when you use your Inner Observer (Practice 3) to compassionately witness your inner critic? Do you find you have more choice in responding rather than reacting to the critic's storyline? Explain.

You've been criticizing yourself for years and it hasn't worked.
Try approving of yourself and see what happens.

—Louise L. Hay, American motivational speaker and author

Half-Truths We Tell Ourselves

A half-truth is even more dangerous than a lie. A lie, you can detect at some stage, but half a truth is sure to mislead you for long.

—Anurag Shourie, *Half a Shadow*

Depending on our Ennea-type and our level of self-realization, we tend to buy into certain half-truths—namely, propositions that might *sometimes* be applicable but end up becoming limiting life paradigms when we apply them as *universally* true.

Reflect on your relationship with the following concepts, focusing on the ones for your type. How often have you heard yourself saying them, whether out loud or in your head? How might your belief in those ideas be limiting you?

Activation by Type

e1:

I always have to do everything myself.
(I can't ever get quality help.)

e2:

I can never let my loved ones down.
(I'll tend to my own needs after I'm finished helping them.)

e3:

After I accomplish this next goal, I'll be happy.
(I'm almost there. Just one more thing to do.)

e4:

No one truly understands me—or the depth of my suffering.
(I must be alone with my darkness.)

e5:

I prefer to watch (and critique) from the sidelines.

(I don't really care to participate anyway.)

e6:

Worrying is how I keep myself and those I care about safe.

(To relax would be irresponsible and uncaring.)

e7:

It's 100 percent better to avoid painful feelings than to suffer through them.

(Only fools—or the unimaginative—suffer gladly.)

e8:

I can't ever rely on other people.

(After all, if I let my guard down, I'll get burned. If I become dependent, I'll be controlled.)

e9:

I don't want to ever stand out or make waves.

(I'd rather just stay under the radar.)

Reflect: Consider the opening quotation from Anurag Shourie. Have you found this to be true in your experience? If so, when? Each of these propositions does something that keeps your sense of separateness intact. How does the proposition for your type reinforce your perspective on the nature of life and your role in it?

Don't believe everything you think.

—Robert Fulghum, *All I Really Need to Know I Learned in Kindergarten*

Grieving Life Passages

When something dies is the greatest teaching.

—Shunryu Suzuki, *Zen Mind, Beginner's Mind*

One of the most fundamental truths of our human experience is the reality of change. While change itself is a universal constant, certainly seasons of change can feel more uprooting than others—for example, change that occurs after the loss of a loved one, upon a serious medical diagnosis, or at the end of a relationship or career. Such life passages can open a floodgate of grief and a profound sense of disorientation.

Be sure to investigate your community and expert resources if you are experiencing complicated grief or trauma, as this Enneagram activation work is by no means a substitute for proper mental health care, grief counseling, or other professional support. In fact, I recommend that if you are questioning the degree of your grief, seek expert guidance before applying this activation.

For this activation, we focus on the fact that it can be tempting to try to bypass the pain of loss. Ultimately, it doesn't serve us to run from our pain. We can only heal by entering into it more fully—living *through* our loss. Remember:

Absence is not remedied by distractions or distance.

Absence is healed by presence.

If we are willing to not feel so in control, if we are willing to feel the tough feelings, if we are willing to embrace our unique experience and not tell ourselves stories about how we should be over this or that loss by now, then, oh, the gifts that are in store for us! The following activation offers just a few suggestions tailored to each Ennea-type for how we each might bring greater kindness and consciousness to our life's most significant passages. These are not meant to encompass the totality of your grief or transition experience. Whatever you might be going through, may this life transition bring about life-giving transformation.

Activation by Type

e1: Amid grief, loss, or transition, recognize that it's okay to feel out of control and let certain things fall by the wayside to make space for processing your thoughts and feelings. When it comes to upper body tension, which is common for you, remember to physically shake it off or get a massage. If you are feeling especially irritable, controlling, or angry, check to see if you're also feeling fear, shame, sadness, or resentment. See if you can sink into the deeper feelings that lie beneath the surface feelings. Recognize that none of these feelings are right or wrong. Remember that there isn't just one right or proper way to grieve or to let go.

e2: Amid grief, loss, or transition, forgo the temptation to focus on others' needs for comfort or support while neglecting your own. Be willing to feel your own challenging feelings around the situation, especially any anger, guilt, resentment, or even relief that might arise. It can be difficult to admit at first, but it is quite healing to recognize that when a person or situation you cherish brings up mixed emotions (and most do), then so would their loss. Resist your tendency to fill up all your spare time helping others so that you have no time left for your own healing. Though it might feel selfish to do so, choose a soothing self-care activity, such as yoga or a restorative bath.

e3: Amid grief, loss, or transition, resist staying busy to avoid negative feelings such as hurt, sadness, and shame, which can seem unnecessarily debilitating to you. If you can't be still, then use your energy to create a personalized private letting go ritual, such as a burning bowl ceremony, to help you with your grief process. Let your feelings out as much as you need to, even if it feels silly or embarrassing. In the end, trust that you're going to be okay not by avoiding your challenging emotions but rather by embracing them. It can feel paradoxical, yet when it comes to healing, your willingness to slow way down speeds your healing way up.

e4: You are all too familiar with grief, loss, and sadness. What can deeply support your journey toward wholeness is doing something physical with your body, such as dance, yoga, or horseback riding. Also, remember to look for beauty right in front of you. Attention to the present moment can help you anchor into your life today so that you don't get swept out to sea by the current of what has recently or long since passed. Finally, while it might feel necessary to withdraw and listen to your favorite songs for a while, remember that you are nourished by interacting with and thinking about others, which helps you to feel a greater sense of belonging with the people in your life right here and right now.

e5: The experience of transition, grief, and loss can feel overwhelming. When stressed, you might tend to hold your breath, both literally and figuratively. Notice how you contract your energy. Remember to pause and take deep breaths, taking your sweet time on the inhale and even longer on the exhale. Do your best to stay engaged and openhearted. Connect with your feelings and share them with one or more trustworthy individuals. It might also be helpful to reminisce with others, sharing important memories relating to your loss. Make peace with uncertainty. Finally, do your best to get some exercise. Easy, repetitive movement can feel particularly comforting and healing to you.

e6: When experiencing grief, loss, or transition, it is vital to take breaks to drop from your head into your body. For instance, walk, bike, work in the yard, or cook. Better yet, practice these activities mindfully, noticing the sensation of your body and the temperature of the air as you move. Giving your mind a break is essential to it functioning with less worry and more effectiveness. Don't forget to be kind to yourself. Moreover, recognize that if you're feeling guilt or anger, you're likely to project such feelings onto others and become overly suspicious that they are against you rather than there to support you.

e7: When experiencing transition, grief, or loss, be aware of your tendency to positively reframe the situation or to find pleasant distractions to avoid negative feelings. Stay in the present moment as best you can. Notice *all* feelings but especially any sadness, fear, or anxiety, and what those feel like in your body. Bringing conscious awareness to physical sensations in your body will help ground you in the present. While negative feelings can feel as if they will go on forever, trust that the sooner you sink into them, the sooner they will move through you. In contrast, the more you resist, the more they'll follow you everywhere.

e8: Loss can feel like a punch in the gut. You might feel betrayed—if not by a particular person, then by life itself! You may want to go out and make someone pay for your pain, go home and withdraw into your cave, or both. This is the place where your rugged individualism can deteriorate into calloused isolation-ism. More vulnerable feelings of hurt, betrayal, or rejection can arise only to be quickly masked by rage. During any major life transition, grief, or loss, seek out support from a trusted loved one. A sturdy shoulder, listening ear, or all-enveloping hug can do wonders—but only when you're willing to submit to tender care!

e9: Amid grief, loss, or transition, you don't tend to act out; rather, you act in. Instead of lashing out at life, you tend to hunker down into what can readily become a black pit of despair. Expressing your feelings through art or move-ment can be an invaluable saving grace. Be willing to not just demonstrate harmony and poignancy in your creative activities. Be willing to also express your agitation and anger. Let yourself be fierce and fiery as well as wobbly and watery in your healing journey.

Reflect: What insights have you gained about your relationship to transition, grief, or loss? How have transition times in your life been transformational for you?

If you are in the throes of a significant loss or transition, please remember to take stock of your internal and external resources. There is no need to process everything on your own. How might you reach out for additional support (or lean further into the support you already have)?

All changes, even the most longed for, have their melancholy;
for what we leave behind us is a part of ourselves; we must
die to one life before we can enter into another.

—Anatole France, French poet and journalist

Mental Exams and Cleaning

A disciplined mind leads to happiness,
and an undisciplined mind leads to suffering.

—Dalai Lama XIV, *The Art of Happiness*

We all know that the longer we delay obtaining routine medical and dental exams and check-ups, the worse our physical health is likely to get. Similarly, to the extent we neglect to periodically examine the health of our own consciousness, our psychological, emotional, and spiritual health can deteriorate. Without regular "consciousness check-ups," we can lapse into injurious or even self-destructive mental and emotional states without even realizing it. We can get so acclimated to these states that we may not fully recognize the degree to which our wellbeing has diminished until we get a harsh wake-up call.

Centering Prayer (Practice 1) is a powerful spiritual practice recommended as a daily or twice-daily routine to support alignment with our highest self. If you haven't already taken up this practice, now might be a great time! Additionally, the following activation is designed to encourage regular "consciousness check-ups" throughout the day to keep our Ennea-types' limiting beliefs from undermining our lives.

Activation by Type

e1: Today, I check my "stinking thinking." Since my default is noticing what's gone wrong, I practice noting and naming what is right. I focus on gratitude for the people and things I have been disregarding or overlooking.

e2: Today, I check my pride. Where I catch myself assuming I know what's best for someone else, I back off on giving unsolicited advice and trust that each person has a unique path. I focus on my own joys and challenges.

e3: Today, I check my speed. Where I find myself just trying to check off the boxes as quickly as possible, I slow down and mindfully attend to each moment of my day. I focus on being *here* rather than getting *there*.

e4: Today, I check my envy. Where I find myself lost in comparisons and longing, I remember to throw myself a lifeline of self-love and affirmation. Grounded in my own fortitude, I powerfully embody the true love I've been waiting for!

e5: Today, I check my hoarding. Having enough space, energy, and privacy are vital to my wellbeing, but the reality is that I often have more to give than my mind tells me I do. When I practice believing I have enough and I *am* enough, I feel more energy to share my life with others.

e6: Today, I check my fears. Where I find myself suspicious or mistrustful of those whom I normally trust, I remember that I'm more likely to project ill will onto others when I am feeling critical or self-doubting. I give myself a reassuring hug and a break!

e7: Today, I check my mental space. If it feels like I have too many search tabs open in my head with too many new ideas and incomplete projects, I close multiple ones down just for now. I focus on just one or two plans or processes at a time.

e8: Today, I check my tendency to think in terms of "us versus them." Where I see myself defaulting to an offensive or defensive position, I take a step back and evaluate the gray areas. I try to not merely understand intellectually but to feel into the psychological and emotional nuances of all perspectives.

e9: Today, I check my tendency to withdraw. I ask myself: *Is my seclusion self-loving and life-giving or is it taking me further into my idealizations and despair—and away from everyday reality?*

Reflect: What, if anything, surprised you when you did your check-ups? Did you see any patterns of thinking or feeling that were new to you or that you did not previously realize that you engaged in so regularly?

Do you have a regular spiritual practice? If so, what does it look like? Did you experiment with incorporating Centering Prayer (Practice 1) into your daily routine? If so, how is that going for you?

> *The person who constantly studies without doing spiritual practice*
> *is like the fool who attempts to live in the blueprint of a house.*

—Mata Amritanandamayi (aka "Amma"), Indian Hindu spiritual leader

Forgiving Yourself

*Self-rejection is the greatest enemy of the spiritual life because
it contradicts the sacred voice that calls us the "Beloved."*

—Henri Nouwen, *Life of the Beloved*

*We all make mistakes, don't we? But if you can't forgive
yourself, you'll always be an exile in your own life.*

—Curtis Sittenfeld, American writer

Forgiving ourselves is not about refusing to take responsibility for our actions. In fact, it is vital to take whatever outer steps we can to make amends and rectify past harms. Self-forgiveness *as an inner act*, however, is an essential part of the spiritual journey. No matter how hard we might wish or pray for it, we cannot access Divine Love if we are the very ones punishing ourselves. Love cannot abide where it is not welcomed.

Indeed, taking personal responsibility for how we show up does not mean we ever need to lock our souls up in a self-made purgatory or exile our hearts from Divine Grace and human belonging. This activation is about embracing the irrevocable truth that your essence is whole and good, and every fiber of your being is worthy of love and forgiveness. Resolve in this moment to set yourself free to live and to love more open-heartedly so you can more fully experience and express Divine Love through-out the remainder of your precious and sacred lifetime.

Activation by Type

e1: No one gets everything right. No one does everything perfectly. Do not punish yourself for being human. Send more love and compassion to yourself when you discover that you've erred, not less! Be a place of peace for yourself, not an enabler of domestic inner violence.

e2: It is not your job to make everyone happy. It is not reasonable to expect everyone to like you. Yet when important relationships aren't as strong or positive as you would like them to be, you take on more than your share of blame and responsibility. Do your best to let this go.

e3: Until you forgive yourself, you'll spend the rest of your days—and nights—overcompensating for where you feel you have failed. As you drive yourself harder and harder, you can tend to end up further and further away from your true path. Forgive yourself so you can welcome the full worthiness of who you are today and not keep looking for it in the future.

e4: What you most need to forgive in yourself isn't one thing or another that you did; rather, it's who you are (or think you are). You have condemned and shamed yourself from the beginning. Give yourself a new start. Forgive yourself for who you thought you should be or might have been. Find your voice and power in fully embracing all the characteristics as well as the essence of who you are in this moment today.

e5: You tend to harbor resentment toward anyone who has seemed to reject you. It is as if by rejecting them, you spare yourself the doubt and misgiving around how you were critiqued. If you make them smaller or more stupid by condemning them, then they have no authority to judge you. Notice what you have not yet forgiven in yourself. Likely it has to do with an area in which you feel fearful or incompetent. If someone else has triggered you, chances are that before you can forgive them, you need to release this high expectation of your own capabilities.

e6: No amount of vigilance can possibly keep everyone you love, including you, safe. Yet when harm occurs, whether inadvertently by your personal actions or by an external cause you didn't foresee, you often judge yourself harshly. Letting the Ghost of Mistakes Past haunt and torment you is inhumane. Moreover, it only fuels more anxiety and second-guessing, which disempowers you from making wise and compassionate decisions in the present and for the future. Set yourself free from the shackles of the past.

e7: If you are on a path of self-awareness, chances are you are realizing all the dreams you have sabotaged, the bridges you've burned, and the love that you have been too afraid to lean into. The fact that it is darkest before the dawn applies to your inner, as well as the outer, horizon. Your willingness to stay with the darkness—to feel your own fears, anger, resentment, or grief deep in your heart and bones—and not hastily move on, allows you to experience the dawning of a truly new and transformed life.

e8: Do not confuse moving on with letting go. Forgive yourself the big dreams that never fully materialized, the people you couldn't help, and the important situations you could not control. Your vision and appetite for bigness is a gift but it is also a heavy burden. There is power you can claim in the present when you get real about what happened in the past. Bring compassionate strength to all that you have not yet grieved so you can finally let go.

e9: When you finally wake up to parts of yourself that went to sleep—whether for weeks, months, or years—you can tend to be hard on yourself. Do not judge yourself for what you weren't ready to see or know or act on until now. Weep if you need to for your old self and life, but don't condemn yourself. This will only make you want to go back into hiding. Resist your tendency toward inertia. Coax yourself out further with self-forgiveness and loving-kindness.

Reflect: Did you find that you could forgive yourself? If not, then consider what is truly in the way of your self-forgiveness? Ask yourself: *How does my unforgiveness serve me? What does it help me to do? What does it protect me from? What do I fear will happen if I forgive myself?* Self-forgiveness becomes easier once we realize that compassion can help us respond more skillfully to life than unforgiveness can.

Feeling compassion for ourselves in no way releases us from responsibility for our actions. Rather, it releases us from the self-hatred that prevents us from responding to our life with clarity and balance.

—Tara Brach, American psychologist and author

DAY 9

The Strength in Softness

*You know that soft is stronger than hard, water
stronger than rocks, love stronger than force.*

—Hermann Hesse, *Siddhartha*

In the following activation, you are invited to enlist a gentle, yet persistent, approach to effecting change in your daily life. The focus is not so much on *what* as *how*: show up softly. Be tender yet devoted in your attitude toward everything you're seeking to do or have, and then see what happens.

Activation by Type

e1: I remember to relax my shoulders and soften my gaze. I meet life's challenges with suppleness and flexibility. Letting go of the idea that there's just one "right" way to proceed is an act of faith that makes sacred space for miracles and grace.

e2: I notice where I can be stubborn in insisting that I be perceived in a positive way by the important people in my life. Inwardly, this means being more open to accepting people as they are and not as I wish them to be. Outwardly, it also means being firmer in showing my truth, rather than hiding my more "negative" feelings or traits to gain others' approval.

e3: I remember not to treat my body like a machine. My body is not just a piece of equipment to be used to accomplish my goals. In truth, it is a temple of my spirit; it is an aspect of divinity made incarnate. I bring tenderness and devotion to any hurt or tired parts of me today.

e4: I reject the notion that I am "too much." I am exactly who I need to be. Today, I act on my inmost truth as a way of honoring my unique gifts and boundless creativity.

e5: I relax my mind and remember to do something physical that gets me into my body. Whether it is playing a sport, creating art, or taking a Tai Chi class, the point is not whether I feel competent at it but whether the activity is enjoyable and energizing.

e6: I let my mind take a breather as I engage in physical activity that is both strengthening and grounding. Whether it is gardening or lifting weights, I focus on feeling the pure sensations that arise in my body as I move. Trying my best to do so without self-judgment, I notice the feel of my hands and feet and the pull of gravity as I sit or stand, squat or twirl, walk or skip.

e7: I spend a few minutes becoming aware of my breathing, visualizing my inhale and exhale gently going right through my heart center. As I focus on my heart, I take long, deep breaths and notice any feelings that arise within me. Whether positive or negative, I warmly welcome them all.

e8: I remember to check in with parts of me that might feel uncertain, powerless, anxious, or vulnerable. I do not try to power through these feelings or concerns but include them in my self-care efforts and future planning. It is when I ignore my humanness and act as if I'm invincible that I am weaker, less resilient, and more likely to sabotage my dreams.

e9: I remember to activate my energy through vigorous activity. While I might be drawn to peaceful, flowing movements, it is harsh, often anaerobic exercise that helps me to get in contact with repressed emotions such as fear or anger. When I can soften my resistance to my own anger and honor these feelings energetically, it helps me to become more authentically powerful and peaceful.

Reflect: How has the practice of softening changed you?

> *There is nothing as strong as tenderness,*
> *And nothing as tender as true strength.*

—Saint Francis de Sales, Catholic theologian

Surf the Urge

You can't stop the waves, but you can learn to surf.

—Jon Kabat-Zinn, mindfulness teacher

Urge surfing is a mental technique you can use to observe and experience an urge without engaging in it. Psychologist Alan Marlatt developed the concept to help in addiction recovery.[2] For this practice, when you have an urge to do something that does not serve your highest good, follow the steps described in this activation. Also, read the activation for your Ennea-type and reflect on when the motivation behind your urges might be personality-driven and not always obviously problematic since your type tells you: *This is good. This is what I want—and why don't others see it this way too?* The compulsion to behave in this way is driven by your egoic self and not your divine nature.

Don't be limited to the suggestions in your type's activation. They are just that—*suggestions*. Use these to help you to be aware of times when your immediate reaction to distress is to reach for a behavior that merely numbs rather than expresses your most authentic and faith-filled being. Urges usually peak at twenty to thirty minutes. Remember to be gentle on yourself and surf the wave.

Steps to Urge Surfing

STEP 1: Sense the urge.

Don't fight with yourself or with the urge. Instead, notice where you feel the urge in your body, then drop into the physical sensation of it. Notice its location in the body. Does it have a weight, temperature, shape, or color? Stay there for five to ten minutes.

STEP 2: Shift your attention.

Consciously shift your attention to your breath for about five minutes. You might want to say to yourself "inbreath, outbreath" as you breathe. Focus on sending your inbreath to the part of your body feeling the urge to act.

STEP 3: Ride the wave.

Notice how the urge can come in waves. See if you can physically sense those waves and just ride them until they dissipate.

STEP 4: Thank yourself!

Thank yourself for this self-loving effort. Urge surfing will get easier with practice.

Activation by Type

e1: Surf the urge to clean or organize everything before you make time for rest or play today. Experiment with doing the "easy" thing first (or in between responsibilities) even though what's "easy" may feel much harder for you to do.

e2: Surf the urge to proactively reach out to someone who historically hasn't taken the initiative to check in or support you. Be willing to receive even half as much as you give, even though this can feel ultra-uncomfortable to do.

e3: Surf the urge to strive for your worth every second of your day. Imagine yourself reclining into the now and noticing what you might do in this moment or the rest of today if you simply assumed you are worthy and already more than enough.

e4: Surf the urge to adjust your appearance to be perceived as special or different. Allow yourself space to just "be" even when it feels uncomfortable and even shameful to blend in or feel "normal."

e5: Surf the urge to go down yet another rabbit hole of obscure information so that you preserve your time and energy to be fully attentive to people who matter most to you.

e6: Surf the urge to be suspicious and to repudiate, inwardly or outwardly, any positive feedback. Open your mind and heart to believing and taking in affirmation and kindness from others, even though it can intensify feelings of fear and vulnerability.

e7: Surf the urge to be constantly stimulated by new ideas or plans, which always hold promise but never actual fulfillment. What might feel at first like unbearable boredom amid your inner silence will ultimately transform into heartfelt joy.

e8: Surf the urge to create a sense of aliveness or intensity through poking or provoking others, which creates a thicker callousness around your own sensitivities. Resist confrontation consistently enough to feel your own heart grow softer toward others and more tender toward yourself.

e9: Surf the urge to overaccommodate just to keep the peace. By resisting this habit of self-censorship, you make space for true belonging, which does not require self-abnegating conformity.

Reflect: Did you learn anything new about your urges? How often were you able to surf the urge? Were you able to be compassionate even when you gave into any of them? If you were not, did you notice whether your urges amplified or diminished under your judgmental gaze? Know that every time you *can* urge surf, the strength of your compulsive urge diminishes.

> *Every time you close another door—be it the door of immediate satisfaction, the door of distracting entertainment, the door of busyness, the door of guilt and worry, or the door of self-rejection—you commit yourself to go deeper into your heart and thus deeper into the heart of [Love].*
>
> —Henri Nouwen, *The Inner Voice of Love*

The Voice for Love

The Voice for Love is always calling to us. It tells us God's Will,
which is to be and extend Love. [Divine Love's] Voice
comes to us in peace, for that is Love's innate condition.

—Pathways of Light[3]

If we have an inner critic, why not also have an inner encourager, a stalwart cheer-leader, a trustworthy mentor? If Love is our nature, why is Love not also our closest companion, our dearest friend, our inner "soulmate," the voice of Truth inside us?

Too many of us have become accustomed to allowing the inner voices of shame, fear, mistrust, and sometimes even spite and hate dictate our lives. At the end of the day, rather than letting these voices take charge, why not let the gentler voice that speaks on behalf of Love be the one that governs, the one we check in with, and the one we curl up with?

The voice for Love does not yell, scream, or berate. We hear its gentle whispers only in silence and stillness. What questions might the Beloved ask of each of us, according to our type's greatest needs? The following activation is intended to support you in absorbing words of Love. Take a moment to be still and listen for the voice of gentleness inside you, whispering encouragement, faith, and hope, letting you know that you are whole, worthy, and enough.

Activation by Type

e1: What did you set down?

e2: How were you nurtured?

e3: What feels authentic and true?

e4: What did you appreciate?

e5: What moved you?

e6: When did you let go?

e7: What satisfied you?

e8: How were you gentle?

e9: Do you matter to yourself?

Reflect: How did you respond to the voice of Love as expressed in the inquiry for your type? Were you kinder and gentler with yourself this week?

> *Today we can set aside this voice of fear and welcome the Voice*
> *of Love. As we welcome this Voice, we learn to recognize the Self*
> *that extends Love without limit. We practice stepping back from*
> *engaging in the world's chaos to settle into Love. In peace, we*
> *awaken to our eternal Home in Love's oneness.*
>
> —Pathways of Light[4]

Self-Restraint

Sometimes our power resides not in what we do, but in what we don't do.

—Paulo Coelho, author of *The Alchemist*

The following activation is about resisting our habitual type patterns so that new ways of being—and of thriving—can emerge. By exercising self-restraint, we make space for a power greater than ourselves to express itself throughout our lives.

Activation by Type

e1: The stress of seeing and shouldering all that might be improved in this world can knock you down physically and emotionally. Before you declare defeat, place your entire burden before the altar of the Divine. Let Infinite Wisdom return to you only the responsibilities that were legitimately yours in the first place.

e2: Feeling thwarted in your ability to help someone you cherish can bring up feelings of desperation or worthlessness. Letting yourself lovingly accept your own human limitations is the beginning of feeling the true humility that brings you closer to Divine Love.

e3: If you're not planning way ahead, you tend to feel way behind. Surrender any sense of urgency about getting anywhere other than where you are today. Take deep breaths, focusing on your heart center. Invite yourself to trust that you are worthy based on who you *are*—and not the person you are striving to be. You are exactly where you need to be.

e4: Stop abandoning yourself by buying into the cheap and easy label that you are "broken." No matter what you have been through, you have *always* been Divine and Whole. What if you lived today with a grateful heart and just *assumed* this to be true?

e5: There is a resource of energy, ideas, and passion that can be experienced in relationship. Cultivating your heart's capacity to receive this storehouse takes practice. Make the effort to connect with someone, through a phone call or kind gesture. Reach out today rather than just reaching in.

e6: Your gift of scanning for threats and dangers can blind you to the wide-open fields of your own flourishing. Take breaks from fortifying your life and dare to delight in the simple joys that are familiar or that have newly blossomed.

e7: Your lack of focus is a defense mechanism against the threat of pain, boredom, and limitation. But recognize that the need to hop around mentally or physically in every moment is its own prison. Break free of your pattern of inattention and practice bringing your charming self to patiently attend to the here and now.

e8: Your resistance to being controlled can be lifesaving but it can also work against you. Notice what you are automatically rebelling against—which may be quite good for you. Imagine the universe has something amazing in store for you—something exponentially better than what you had planned.

e9: Rest from your distractibility and from your busyness attending to others' agendas so you have energy to focus on your own authentic priorities. Recognize that your gusto for action tends to wane as morning turns to night, so live more fully into your divine potential by consciously releasing inner resistance to your personal priorities; do the harder things first each day.

Reflect: What was it like to exercise restraint in acting out your type pattern? How was this a practice of exercising faith—faith that when the egoic self lets go, there is more space for the indwelling Spirit to be expressed?

Let go and let God.

—Twelve-step slogan

DAY 13

One Day at a Time

One day at a time.

—Alcoholics Anonymous slogan

The phrase *one day at a time* was popularized in twelve-step recovery circles but can readily apply to any change we are trying to make in our lives. It reminds us to focus on the present and what we need to do within the next twenty-four hours. This attitude can cause even lifelong changes to feel doable. Practice this activation for as long as it takes for the activity to become a more customary way for you to be in the world, but approach it just *one day at a time*.

Activation by Type

e1: Just for today, give your inner critic some time off.

e2: Just for today, be willing to ask for help.

e3: Just for today, let yourself savor recent achievements rather than jumping immediately to the next goal or task.

e4: Just for today, practice gratitude not just for others, but for yourself, just as you are.

e5: Just for today, don't try to figure things out by yourself. Ask for input.

e6: Just for today, practice incorporating best-case scenarios into your planning.

e7: Just for today, listen to your heart and not just your head.

e8: Just for today, balance your tendency toward intensity by making time for physical and mental rest.

e9: Just for today, practice speaking your truth, even if others may disagree or disapprove.

Reflect: How did it feel to consider applying your type's activation just for one day at a time? How often might you apply this invitation if you remembered you don't need to keep at it for a lifetime but rather just for today?

> *A journey of a thousand miles begins with a single step.*
>
> —Lao Tzu, ancient Chinese philosopher

Changing Direction

Forward movement is not helpful if
what is needed is a change of direction.

—David Fleming, *Lean Logic*

Each of our Ennea-types has a favored strategy for seeking happiness or wellbeing that sadly misses the mark. For instance, Ones think critiquing and fixing things (and people) will somehow bring them peace. They learn the hard way that this approach only produces ongoing stress and resentment. Ones don't often look for qualities to praise in others, yet often when people feel appreciated, they show up as their highest and best selves. When Ones appreciate their surroundings, they begin to see the good they've been looking for and aren't as overwhelmed by what they deem is bad or wrong. This is just one example.

Activation by Type

e1: Don't underestimate the prospering power of well-placed praise. Whatever you appreciate truly does appreciate!

e2: Don't underestimate the value of *not* thinking about your loved ones, if only for a half hour or two. Make time to do something "just" for you.

e3: Don't underestimate the reward you can feel by challenging yourself to produce absolutely nothing, if only for an evening.

e4: Don't underestimate your capacity to touch the Divine by bringing the caress of rapturous attention to the simplest of everyday chores.

e5: Don't underestimate the comfort you can experience by sharing with another what you feel in your deep and sensitive heart.

e6: Don't underestimate the firm footing you can establish when you gingerly step away from future-tripping.

e7: Don't underestimate the sheer glee you can feel when you pay willing and generous attention to just one moment at a time.

e8: Don't underestimate the strength you can wield when you yield to accepting someone else's gift of care, even if just for a minute.

e9: Don't underestimate the power of your engaged and embodied presence, even if just for the briefest interaction or exchange.

Reflect: How did you react to reading your type's activation? Did the exercise seem insignificant or valuable? Did you apply the suggested practice? If so, did anything shift inside of you? Did anything change in your environment?

> The ego's basic doctrine [is] "Seek but do not find." For what
> could more surely guarantee that you will not find salvation than
> to channelize all your efforts in searching for it where it is not?
>
> —*A Course in Miracles*

Conscious Communication

The great enemy of communication, we find, is the illusion of it.

—William H. Whyte, American sociologist

Do the best you can until you know better.
Then when you know better, do better.

—Maya Angelou, American memoirist and poet

The Enneagram helps us to see the default biases and lenses through which we relate to the world. In my couples and leadership coaching, it is often apparent how even the most self-aware and self-reflective among us do not always perceive how we come across. When we learn to be more aware of our relational tendencies, our communication becomes not only more skillful and effective but also more loving and connecting. These reminders are designed to activate conscious communication.

Activation by Type

e1: Condemning → Encouraging

Watch for how condemnatory you can come across, through your facial expressions, body language, word choice, and tone. Try taking a receptive stance by relaxing your shoulders, unfurrowing your brow, and unclenching your jaw. Scan the situation for what is working or right. Then, using "I" statements, lead your conversation with expressions of gratitude and encouragement, embodying a kinder, more skillful approach to asking for what you want.

e2: Complaining → Requesting

Watch for complaining language and tone as a backward way to solicit acknowledgment and appreciation for your efforts—either by the person you helped or by others. If you need affirmation that you matter, be direct about it. If you need acknowledgment for your sacrifices, be brave and vulnerable enough to own up and ask directly.

e3: Curated → Candid

Watch for how you curate your thoughts and feelings, sharing only the ones you think will gain favorable responses. By doing this, you maintain your image but eliminate any chance for authentic connection. Then you feel the emptiness of never being truly seen for who you are. Speaking candidly, especially about your more negative feelings and embarrassing needs, can feel messy and challenging at first. But it's so worth the inexpert effort for you to allow the possibility of genuine, fulfilling connections.

e4: Wet and Windy → Cut and Dry

Watch for how long-winded, melancholic, and metaphoric you can be in conversations. This tendency can make you a very creative writer and speaker but it is also a way, consciously or unconsciously, you render your audience captive to whatever state you're in. It can also sabotage your relationship goals by obscuring what you're really wanting. It's perfectly wonderful to feel deeply and want to communicate meaningfully. However, the connection you long for can more readily happen when you balance emotional sharing with clear and concise statements—as well as practical requests your loved ones can act upon.

e5: Cross → Caring

Watch for how you spontaneously challenge new information either with cold containment or cross confrontation. While it is true that unsubstantiated opinions are the bane of your existence, recognize that behind some sharing lies much more than the substance of the information shared. Consider that the exchange of information is often about connecting with one another's shared humanity. Become curious about the person sharing the information. Why might these facts or this story be important to them? Are they really interested in the weather or in spending time together? Are they wanting you to opine on what they're reporting, or do they simply want someone to join in their excitement for a new activity or discovery?

e6: Concern → Confidence

Watch for how your care and compassion can come across as over-weighty concern or outright contrariness. This energy can feel bubble-bursting and defeating to others who might be sharing a new and exciting idea or plan with you that already feels quite fragile in its infancy. Bring your natural sense of warmth to meet the moment. It's okay to feel your concern but try leading with faith, hope, and confidence and then see if they want your safety advice. They might say "yes" and then tell you when it might be a better time to share your counsel and information.

e7: Sampling → Savoring

Watch for your mental carelessness and capriciousness, unloading extraordinary amounts of data on a person at once, then changing the subject without finishing your last sentence. You don't always realize how your capacious energy and appetite for new ideas and possibilities leaves others both overfull and unsatisfied. Slow down and savor the juiciness of your own conversation and pay closer attention to your conversation companions. What might *they* be feeling or experiencing? How might you go deeper together in this shared space?

e8: Blunt → Discerning

Watch for how you use directness as a weapon: "I'm just being honest" is not an excuse for being cruel. Your penchant for unmoderated bluntness is especially unfair given how, if you're honest with yourself, you are fairly sensitive deep down—especially when it comes to feedback from the people you care about. Take time to discern your true motives for communicating. Does it come from even the slightest desire to retaliate or to manipulate the situation to better meet your goals? When and how (if ever) does this opinion of yours need to be shared so that it can be most fully and effectively heard? How might you focus on opening to more honest, authentic, openhearted connections and less on maintaining control?

e9: Toning It Down → Speaking Up

Watch out for your tone policing, which is one way you make others' intensity the culprit in a conversation when the issue is more likely the product of your chemistry together. Try not to tell someone they're "too much" or that they must "tone it down." The issue isn't them per se but how you are responding to them.

Own your part by speaking in "I" statements, acknowledging your tendency to shut down or become small amid others' intense energy or emotions. Use statements such as "When you get loud, I shut down. I want to be able to hear you," or "when emotions are high, I feel overwhelmed, and I struggle to discern what feelings are mine."

Reflect: What did you learn about your communication tendencies? What about those of other types? How has this activation impacted your ability to connect more authentically and skillfully with others?

> *A real conversation always contains an invitation.*
> *You are inviting another person to reveal herself or himself*
> *to you, to tell you who they are or what they want.*
>
> —David Whyte

Silence, Solitude, and Stillness

There is nothing as certain as silence, stillness, and
solitude to introduce you to the secrets of yourself.

—Guy Finley, American writer and philosopher

The contemplative postures of silence, stillness, and solitude are aptly referred to as the *trinity of contemplation* given their necessity to our inner journey. When we begin, it is easiest to start with *external* silence, stillness, and solitude. We might take time away from our families and friends, silence our cell phones, and sit down under a tree or on our meditation cushion. Eventually, we cultivate an *interior* silence, stillness, and solitude—a kind of sacred inner space, a quietude, a clearing, or even a light within ourselves that we find persists even amid the bustle of everyday life. This starts to feel like a place we come from rather than just a place we go to when we meditate.

One helpful way of thinking about these three contemplative postures is that it is not so much about retreating *away from* the world's noise, people, or activity. Rather, it can be more helpful to think about it as being devotedly silent, solitary, and still *toward* the Divine.

Interior silence, solitude, and stillness are helpful to everyone on a path of awakening, irrespective of Enneagram type. However, in *The Sacred Enneagram*, Christopher L. Heuertz illuminates how each of these are acutely valuable for each of the Enneagram intelligence centers:

- *Inner stillness* invites body types (Types 8, 9, and 1) to "[slow] down the initiating energy that drives gut people, creating a sacred pause that nurtures accountable action."

- *Inner solitude* can be particularly life-affirming for heart types (Types 2, 3, and 4) by "[allowing] for a deep experience of being loved, thereby helping heart people find their inner source of love for the world."

- *Inner silence* can be especially grounding for head types (Types 5, 6, and 7) "to arrest their mental obsessions and cultivate quiet to achieve a grounded peace."[5]

The following activation offers suggestions on how you might infuse contemplative silence, solitude, or stillness into your day based on your type and its recommended contemplative posture. Consider using these ideas to craft your personal contemplative retreat as well. Note that Centering Prayer (see Practice 1) is recommended for fostering inner silence, solitude, and stillness across persons of *all* types.

Activation by Type

e1: To practice contemplative *stillness*, I experience profound restoration by infusing sacred moments of rest throughout my day. (If helpful, I set a timer every few hours to remind myself to stop, become still, and simply *be*—if only for a half a minute each time.)

e2: To practice contemplative *solitude*, I carve out solitary space that no one else is allowed to interrupt to do something I personally enjoy, such as a hobby or creative activity. (I might intentionally select an activity that feels indulgent simply because I would be doing it "just" for *me!*)

e3: To practice contemplative *solitude*, I make an appointment with myself. I set aside distractions and mindfully engage with my innermost self, being curious about who I am and how I feel. (If needed, I schedule this time on my calendar. If helpful, I get out in nature.)

e4: To practice contemplative *solitude*, during my alone time, I intentionally rest from mental fantasies, embracing the exquisite experience of the real that is here now, rather than the mirage of the unattainable ideal.

e5: To practice contemplative *silence*, I willingly take short pauses from observing and learning about the external world and patiently inquire into the quiet mysteries of my own heart.

e6: To practice contemplative *silence*, I routinely soften my gaze and touch base with the ground beneath me, giving myself permission to relax my vigilance.

e7: To practice contemplative *silence*, I take deep breaths to create a spoke in the fast-moving wheel of my own thinking. I slow down enough to let my heart catch up with my head.

e8: To practice contemplative *stillness*, I willingly restrain myself from instinctively charging forward every chance I get and instead say "yes" more often to becoming inwardly silent and still.

e9: To practice contemplative *stillness*, I pause and resist the urge to flow down the riverbed grooves carved by others. After pausing, I boldly redirect my course and take engaged action, stepping decisively in the direction of my authentic path.

Reflect: What is your relationship to silence, stillness, and solitude? Which of these is hardest for you? What scares you about this depth of contemplation? What benefits have you experienced when you have made more space for them? Did this inspire ways to incorporate more contemplative practice into your life?

> *Contemplation is a very dangerous activity. It not only brings*
> *us face to face with God. It brings us, as well, face to face with*
> *the world, face to face with the self. And then, of course,*
> *something must be done. Nothing stays the same once we have*
> *found the God within. . . . We carry the world in our hearts.*

—Joan D. Chittister, American nun and theologian

Offsetting Your Ennea-Type Tendencies

The heart of the story is clear: each of us is in prison. We have only to awaken to "read" the pattern of the lock that will allow us to escape.

—Don Riso and Russ Hudson, *The Wisdom of the Enneagram*

By intentionally offsetting our type tendencies, we build new muscles of attention and behavior. We are freer to show up in more skillful and adaptive ways that express our authentic desires. One day at a time, we can chip away at the prison of type.

Activation by Type

e1: Today, I release the perception that it is up to me to fix everything.

e2: Today, I practice setting better boundaries around my time and energy.

e3: Today, I make space for feelings—my own and others'.

e4: Today, I feel a sense of power and meaning from taking concrete action on my dreams.

e5: Today, I engage and connect with others even when I don't feel I have all the information or expertise I'd like.

e6: Today, I make independent and firm decisions for myself.

e7: Today, I experience the joy of helping someone else out.

e8: Today, I practice listening, recognizing that I'll learn more if I don't always talk or direct a conversation.

e9: Today, I take initiative on an idea or project. I practice leading rather than just going along with others.

Reflect: Reflect on your experience offsetting one of your type's tendencies. What might happen if you kept at this one practice for an entire year?

What you took as yourself begins to look like a little prison-house far away in the valley beneath you.

—Gurdjieff

Building Bridges

People are lonely because they build walls instead of bridges.

—Joseph Fort Newton, American author

Learning about our Ennea-types, we come to see ways we may unwittingly block the very love and nurturing we seek. Some of us tend to do it aggressively, others more defensively. This activation is about recognizing how staying fixated in our type patterns can directly sabotage the care and connection we need.

Activation by Type

e1: Recognize that when you're hypercritical of others, your relationship is not a safe space in which they can grow, heal, or transform. Don't turn your personal need for orderliness, for instance, into a universal principle or proclamation about how others should or should not be. Trust that speaking in "I" statements about what you're feeling and needing is a substantially more effective, kinder way to get your needs met than simply telling your loved ones all the things they did, or are doing, wrong.

e2: Realize it is not reasonable or fair to expect loved ones to be able to read your mind or anticipate your needs, especially when you yourself don't often recognize what you're desiring or needing. Checking in with yourself and then asking directly for what you want is a courageous and more loving way to show up in your relationships. You risk getting a "no," but you are also much less likely to harbor (or inspire) resentment—and much more likely to get your needs met.

e3: Recognize that when you seek acknowledgment or affirmation from loved ones regarding something you did well, what you're even more desperately wanting is to know that you are lovable and worthy just for being you. Be willing to admit it if you didn't do something well, especially as it relates to them. Then, even if your mind thinks it's impossible or unreal that you could somehow be worthy amid failure, practice letting yourself feel loved and lovable anyway.

e4: Recognize your tendency to believe that by your suffering and withdrawal, you will somehow draw love to you. Although it is vital that loved ones realize you need space and time to feel your feelings before moving into empowered action, it's also important for you to recognize you need support and encouragement toward the practical execution of your goals. Though it might not feel like it, asking for support in meeting your goals is as important as inviting someone to be present with your feelings.

e5: Recognize your tendency to compartmentalize your feelings, especially when you are overwhelmed. It's okay to withdraw for a time—but don't shut those feelings away indefinitely. Repressing your feelings can hurt relationships. To show up more consciously and skillfully in relationships, be willing to set aside space and time to revisit and to honor your feelings. Then share some of those feelings with the people you care about. Be sure to let them know if you want advice or if you want them to simply sit with you.

e6: Recognize your tendency to test relationships, which can undermine the very stability you seek. After all, you can only poke and prod something for so long before it breaks. Resist the urge to seek continual reassurance and take more routine leaps of faith. Communicate with your loved ones in a manner that assumes they care about and want to support you. Bring more lightness to your interactions by remembering your own wit and clever way of seeing the world. Good-natured humor is a great way for you to bond with others through merriment while taking yourself less seriously.

e7: Recognize that your tendency to be assertive and go after what you want has its strengths, but it can sometimes actually keep you from getting your deeper needs for care and nurturing met. You struggle to let yourself simply sit back and receive others' strength or generosity because you simply don't believe others will even consider what you might need without your prompting. Yet how can anyone offer to meet a need of yours when, by jumping in so quickly and consistently, you leave no space for others' gifts to unfold in their own time?

e8: Recognize that your tendency to be action- rather than communication-oriented can sometimes feel very nonrelational and uncaring to others. You might be doing something spontaneously out of the goodness of your own heart for someone else, but your generous intentions might not be as obvious as you think, as seen from your actions alone. Don't assume people know your heart. Seemingly small gestures such as asking after those you care about, expressing words of affection, and even sharing the intentions behind your loving actions can be some of the biggest gifts you offer.

e9: Recognize that your tendency to not want to make waves by asserting your wants and needs in the moment often results in more long-term harm than good. Be willing to ask for time to make decisions rather than just abnegating relationship decisions to your significant others. You can't be seen, heard, or acknowledged by others if you are constantly hiding or censoring yourself. Showing up and speaking up is not only a powerful act of self-love, but it also shows respect to your loved ones by demonstrating that they are important enough for you to show up authentically and fully.

Reflect: What insights did you gain here about how your Ennea-type impacts your relationships? As you engaged your type's activation, did you see any change in your connections with others?

> *Your task is not to seek for love, but merely to seek and find all the barriers within yourself that you have built against it.*
>
> —Rumi

Triggers

As long as you are defining what you like and what you don't like,
you will open and close. You are actually defining your limits.
You are allowing your mind to create triggers that open and
close you. Let go of that. Dare to be different. Enjoy all of life.

—Michael A. Singer, *The Untethered Soul*

Knowing what consistently triggers us is a helpful entryway into understanding parts of ourselves that we've rejected, repressed, or otherwise shadowed. Often, we have closed off these parts not only from the world but from ourselves. Perceiving and judging those same qualities we don't like as "not me" and only "out there," we tend to focus on trying to control the outer situation, including other people, without ever deeply addressing our own reaction to the people and situation at hand—to pay attention to what it triggers within us.

We tend to condemn in others most harshly and consistently those qualities we are not willing to own in ourselves. For instance, if we are continually triggered by others' apparent incompetence, we might look at whether we habitually and even compulsively act to ensure we never fail or make a single mistake because to do so would bring tremendous inner wrath. Perhaps we might try giving ourselves permission to err as all humans do, without such harsh condemnation.

When you feel triggered, remember to first breathe deeply and bring tremendous self-compassion to your own reactions. Welcoming Prayer (Practice 2) is a great way to wholeheartedly embrace your experience. What if you let yourself relax into one or more of those qualities that you tend to most judge or even abhor?

Activation by Type

e1: When you feel triggered by someone else behaving "badly" or "irresponsibly," check in to see if you have been feeling especially resentful and heavy from being overly self-controlled, responsible, or self-critical. How much of this burden is self-imposed? Ask yourself: *What is this other person doing that I'd like to give myself permission to do, even occasionally?*

e2: When you feel triggered by someone refusing to like you despite your best efforts, check in to see whether you are "giving to get." Conditional giving can feel manipulative to others and even if you do win them over, you are still left wondering if you're only liked or loved for what you have to offer. Ask yourself: *How might I attend to my personal needs as an act of self-love and self-respect?*

e3: When you feel triggered by someone else's inefficiency or incompetence, be honest with yourself about whether you're caring more for your own image or end goal rather than for those around you (including yourself). How might offering patience, support, and a listening ear to yourself and others help you feel happier and more wholehearted? Ask yourself: *What helps me experience the fullness of my own heart?*

e4: When you feel triggered by others not being willing to finish hearing you, check in to see what you want that person to see and affirm about you. What would you witness about yourself if you looked in the mirror and gazed intently into your own eyes? Ask yourself: *What am I wanting others to see that I can see and lovingly affirm in and for myself?*

e5: When you feel triggered by others' emotionality, check in with your body and notice how it can go to a flight, a freeze, and occasionally even a fight response. You tend to take others' feelings as demands and then struggle internally to formulate a competent response. What if you could just let others' feelings be there without having to argue with them, "fix" them, or try to rationalize them away? Ask yourself: *What if others' feelings don't require any kind of expert answer or response and can just be felt in my own heart?*

e6: When you feel triggered by your own mental machinations, check in with yourself to sense your feet on the ground. Then see if you can compassionately witness the spinning of your thoughts without having to spin along with them. Sense the stillness that arises within you when you anchor your attention to the center of all your thoughts and your feelings. Ask yourself: *What inside me is always strong, stable, and steady?*

e7: When you feel triggered by slow talkers, check to make sure you're listening with your heart and leaning in with your body. You tend to hopscotch over other people's sentences (and sometimes your own). What if your agility of thought, which is a gift when brainstorming ideas, is a barrier to true listening? Ask yourself: *What relationship gifts might I be missing out on because I don't slow down and pay full attention with my mind, heart, and body?*

e8: When you feel triggered by injustice, check to make sure you aren't just seeing the situation in black and white. You tend to prefer the underdog, which can blind you to the humanity of the other side. Even if someone committed a wrong, why do you need to see them as so completely evil or corrupt? Ask yourself: *Am I only good or only bad, or do I sometimes harm others and sometimes help them?*

e9: When you feel triggered by conflict, make sure you check your motives for peacemaking. Too often, you justify your accommodating or mediating efforts by assuming everyone else values harmony as much as you do. In truth, others may not be as invested in keeping the peace as you are. They might place a higher priority on speaking their truth or sharing their feelings. It's okay to want peace, but be sure to acknowledge that it's for you that you're seeking it. Ask yourself: *What is it I'm really needing when I'm wanting others to agree or get along?*

Reflect: What came up for you as you explored the activation for your type? What felt challenging for you? What about it was challenging? What felt easy to do? Did your type's suggested practice come easier over time?

Are your desires important enough to make you willing to face your fears? Do you want it bad enough? The choice is yours. You can choose to change your attitude from resignation to commitment, from a state of fear to a state of love. The first step is to question yourself, to literally change your internal statements to questions. Change "I am a failure" to "Could I be a success?" Change "I am bored with my life" to "Could I be exhilarated?" Change "My life doesn't make a difference" to "Could I make a difference in the world?"

—Debbie Ford, *The Dark Side of the Light Chasers*

Rest and Receive

Most of the things we need to be most fully alive
never come in busyness. They grow in rest.

—Mark Buchanan, *The Holy Wild*

To cultivate habits of rest, we must discern what noise has found a
way to penetrate our soul. And as we detect patterns and modes,
we have more of a grounding as we resist restlessness.

—Cole Arthur Riley, *This Here Flesh*

If you are practicing these activations in order, this is our halfway point. Give yourself permission to rest from the tyranny of your type and make peace with how you have showed up. If you need to, practice Welcoming Prayer (Practice 2) and prayerfully surrender your need for power or control, affirmation or approval, certainty or security. Give your personality a break from its 24/7 occupation as your life's manager. Even if it is only a brief recess, grant yourself a reprieve from your personality drivers. Breathe fully into your belly and let your relationship to the indwelling Spirit blossom in this state of rest. Make these words your words, then pause to be still and silent.

Activation by Type

e1: As I willingly receive my breath, I make peace with myself, trusting that even if my efforts seemed imperfect by my high standards, my best truly was good enough.

e2: As I willingly receive my breath, I make time and space to tend to my own needs, reminding myself that this is not selfish. I am as worthy of affection and care as anyone else.

e3: As I willingly receive my breath, I check in with my heart. I treat myself as beloved, no matter what I accomplished or didn't accomplish on this day.

e4: As I willingly receive my breath, I practice gratitude for all that I have, recognizing that my life has its unique challenges and joys—a path authentic to me and incomparable to that of any others.

e5: As I willingly receive my breath, I relax my quest to fully understand or know a particular topic. In this moment, I honor the expertise that I already possess, while granting space for the inevitable unknowns.

e6: As I willingly receive my breath, I remember to bear witness to my own goodness. Often, the loving and protective efforts I make for others are invisible to them, and I let that be okay.

e7: As I willingly receive my breath, I review the past twenty-four hours rather than jumping impatiently to future-planning. I dwell especially on the moments when I experienced joy, contentment, or satisfaction, letting those memories fill my heart.

e8: As I willingly receive my breath, I give myself permission to ask for support. As strong as I am, I am made stronger by the care I'm able to let in.

e9: As I willingly receive my breath, I remember that it's okay to have differences in perspective from those around me. Rather than clamor to make peace, I stay grounded in my own opinions trusting that, even with my differences, I belong.

Reflect: At the end of the day (for each day you choose to engage this activation), practice Welcoming Prayer (Practice 2) and take a brief inventory of your choices, behaviors, and attitudes. To what extent were you able to give yourself a break from your type patterns?

"You have peace," the old woman said, *"when you make it with yourself."*

—Mitch Albom, *The Five People You Meet in Heaven*

A Fresh Perspective

Your assumptions are your windows on the world.
Scrub them off every once in a while, or the light won't come in.

—Alan Alda, American actor, during commencement address

As we engage Enneagram-informed inner work, we come to see more clearly how our type's paradigm reflects but one facet rather than the entire sparkling diamond of reality. Life, as it turns out, is vaster and far more abundant than our type-bound mindsets allow us to experience! Learning your type lens helps you question your assumptions and expand your horizons, empowering you with new options and a fuller perspective for living a life of joy and purpose. This activation is about being open to approaching life from this wider-lens perspective.

Activation by Type

e1: *What if I am most correct when I remember that my truth is but one perspective?*

e2: *What if I am most generous when I can resist calling attention to what I have done for others?*

e3: *What if I am most fulfilled when I make time to cultivate my relationships?*

e4: *What if I am most authentically me when I can find beauty in what is commonplace?*

e5: *What if I am wisest and most capable when I am able and willing to release feelings of powerlessness and hopelessness?*

e6: *What if I am most safe and secure when I am calm, centered, and present to myself?*

e7: *What if I am most happy and content when I can let go of the need to entertain or discuss every new idea or possibility that comes to mind?*

e8: *What if I am most powerfully visionary when I am able and willing to practice patience and compassion, recognizing that true progress need not always leave my companions in the dust?*

e9: *What if I am most loving when I stop procrastinating and take one step outside of my comfort zone toward sharing my gifts with the world?*

Reflect: What came up for you as you reflected on the activation for your type? What happened when you went to implement it?

> *The mind that opens up to a new idea never returns to its original size.*
>
> —Albert Einstein

Forgiving Others

When we think we have been hurt by someone in the past, we build up defenses to protect ourselves from being hurt in the future. So the fearful past causes a fearful future and the past and future become one. We cannot love when we feel fear. . . . When we release the fearful past and forgive everyone, we will experience total love and oneness with all.

—Gerald G. Jampolsky, psychiatrist and founder of Center for Attitudinal Healing

We tend to think forgiveness is about our relationship to the person whom we believe harmed us, or whom we harmed, intentionally or not. True forgiveness, however, is more fundamentally about removing our internal blocks to the presence of love so we can reclaim it in our own hearts. The following activation offers a pathway to removing some of our most typical barriers to embodying and express-ing love based on our respective Ennea-types. Please keep in heart and mind that forgiveness is not about letting someone abuse you or violate your boundaries. True forgiveness is about your *inner* relationship to that person. (It does not even require that the other person still be alive.) Sometimes, forgiveness inspires an outer action—such as a ritual of letting go, making amends, communicating, or even trying to reconcile—but recognize that forgiveness is about shifting toward freedom within consciousness, which happens not by forcing forgiveness but by becoming willing to forgive, at your own pace and in your own time. Sometimes, all we can do is become willing to be willing to forgive.

Activation by Type

e1: The journey of forgiveness requires you to first question your own convic-tion. Your tendency to think in terms of right and wrong can close not only your mind but also your heart. A closed mind cannot see the whole truth. A closed heart cannot love. Pray for compassion, wisdom, and the willingness to see the person or situation differently. Do not force forgiveness and do not resist it. Simply stay open to forgiveness as a movement of grace, which may happen in any holy instant.

e2: To forgive is an act of great humility. When you do so, you recognize that what the other person did (or didn't do) cannot diminish your own worth. Yet you also recognize that your resentful pride is not the proper punishment for the other's crime, whatever its size. Your forgiveness doesn't change your value or theirs. It doesn't necessarily mean you maintain physical connection or communication with the other person. Forgiveness is more an act of soul than body—it is an inner choice that frees your heart to love more fully wherever Divine Wisdom directs your love next.

e3: When important people in your life do not play the role you've ascribed to them, you can feel hostile. How will you keep up your winning role if others mess up their lines or, worse, destroy the entire backdrop to the performance of your life? Healing begins when you honor your feelings, whether you are feeling hurt, disappointment, anger, shame, or grief. Forgiveness happens only after you release the script you think ought to have played out and accept the reality of the way events transpired.

e4: Forgiveness is not about excusing others' behavior. Nor should it ever be a means of invalidating your suffering or pain. Rather, authentic forgiveness is an act of self-love and self-empowerment. Without forgiveness, you invite the past to perpetually wound you. By willingly releasing your attention on the past, you can fully claim your power and wholeness in the present moment. You realize that nothing is missing in the here and now. In truth, you have everything you need to live a thriving and beautiful life.

e5: You tend to hold onto incidents that felt shaming or humiliating. Often, these reflect moments when your deepest fears of incompetency were realized. Somehow you think that your unforgiveness—with its attendant anger, harshness, or coldness toward the persons or institutions involved—protects you from further pain. However, what it mainly does is starve your heart, which requires openness, care, and connection to thrive. Forgiveness is about stepping out from behind your well-guarded emotional fortress because you deserve the freedom to walk unburdened in the world and to experience its many joys.

e6: Your path of forgiveness is helped by realizing that nothing and no one in this world is entirely trustworthy, including yourself. Believing in people and placing faith in them means that sometimes you do experience hurt or betrayal.

Bringing sagacity and compassion to this reality helps you to decide what (or who) is worth the risk of believing in again, and to what degree. It is not about never being hurt again. It is about trusting your intuition to choose interactions wisely and your own strength to bear whatever might come that is beyond your ability to reasonably foresee or control.

e7: When upset, your favored strategy is to cut and run. Don't mistake avoidance of an issue or person as true forgiveness. When you have truly moved on, you don't need to avoid a person or topic so vigilantly. Taking time to reflect on your past hurt or betrayal and embracing your own pain with presence can support you in finding true forgiveness and thus true freedom in your heart.

e8: Generally quick to forgive, you can find it more difficult to forgive when others won't (or can't) honestly admit what they have done. It can feel frustrating and unjust when your pain seems to be so seldom acknowledged by others. Recognize, however, that the willingness to forgive is not for their benefit but for yours. You can let go, simply by refusing to stay connected to that person or issue any longer. Forgiveness is a way for you to take back your own energy and power.

e9: The challenge of forgiveness is realizing you are angry at a person in the first place. This can sometimes occur months or years after an incident. Do not jump too quickly to forgiveness. To authentically forgive, you need to first feel the sense of separation and disunity that comes from owning your judgments and feelings about the person and situation. Where the situation allows, you might also need to first speak your truth before you can move toward true inner peace.

Reflect: Did you feel resistance around this practice? What, if any, emotional, psychological, or physical release did you experience? What insights or blessings did you gain?

> *Out of the forgiveness of others comes self-forgiveness and the*
> *relief of guilt. The real payoff we get is when we let go of our*
> *negativity and choose to be loving; we are the ones who benefit.*
> *We are the ones who gain from the real payoff.*
>
> —David R. Hawkins, *Letting Go*

Tales We Sometimes Tell Ourselves

It is very difficult also to sacrifice one's suffering. A man will renounce any pleasures you like but he will not give up his suffering.

—Gurdjieff

Most of us are not *consciously* holding onto our suffering. We generally believe we are endeavoring to be happier, more faithful, and free. The Enneagram nevertheless helps us to see that part of us, even while wanting change, resists it. Below the surface of our conscious aspirations, we cling to type-driven narratives about what we think we must be or do to be okay. The problem is that this narrative prevents us from ever fully *feeling* okay.

The tales we sometimes tell ourselves are like ill-fitting garments we've outgrown but refuse to stop wearing despite their suffocating and confining limits. The following activation does not purport to tell the whole story of you; yet, hopefully, your type's inquiry gives you a sense of the *fashion* of the garment you are wearing and invites you to consider letting its weave unravel.

Activation by Type

e1: What if you stopped using "I'm my own worst critic" as some badge of honor when it's just a flimsy, self-righteous shield you put up to protect yourself from others' judgment?

e2: What if you stopped thinking self-sacrifice is the highest form of love when it is decidedly prideful to think that Divine Compassion need not embrace you?

e3: What if you stopped assuming others need to see your resume before loving your soul?

e4: What if you stopped thinking others have what you're missing? What if the only thing you're truly missing is seeing the innate beauty and wholeness of who you are?

e5: What if your belief that only intellect can discover or verify "truth" is its own fairy tale? What does your body know? What does your heart tell you?

e6: What if life isn't really meant to be a suspense novel? What if your own story could afford a few grand adventures and some comic relief?

e7: What if your optimism about the future is disguised pessimism about the present moment? What if you trusted that the good you're chronically seeking is always already right under your feet?

e8: What if you stopped seeing everything as a battle, challenge, or contest? What if you'd win more in life by respecting what truly matters instead of constantly fighting what doesn't?

e9: What if reminiscing is not always about honoring the past and is sometimes a polite and convenient means of *self-forgetting* in the present?

Reflect: Did you relate to your type's tale? Did you see the story come up during your practice period with this activation? If so, were you willing to question the truth of your assumptions or beliefs and open to a more expansive view?

Argue for your limitations and, sure enough, they're yours.

—Richard Bach, *Illusions*

Balancing Your Attention

Where attention goes, neural firing flows and neural connection grows.

—Dan Siegel, PhD

Energy follows attention. Wherever your attention goes, your energy follows. This means when attention is unconsciously and habitually focused in one direction, our life energy can become imbalanced. We can unwittingly neglect certain areas of our development and miss out on the fullness of life as well as of our own spiritual whole-ness. When we recognize where we customarily (usually unconsciously) place our attention, we empower ourselves to make new choices. With our conscious replace-ment of attention, we can energize new life pathways.

This activation invites you to catch yourself in type-based habits of attention and to direct your attention toward a more wholistic and balanced view. Remember that what you resist persists, so don't beat yourself up when you catch yourself in type. This only energizes the old, limiting habit of thinking. Instead, gently redirect your mind and entertain an alternative thought.

Activation by Type

e1: *What's praiseworthy?* Notice how often your attention goes toward cutting yourself or others down, whether through petty critiques or harsh condemnation. Balance this by focusing on what is praiseworthy about yourself and others and then consistently and emphatically celebrating all of it!

e2: *What do I really need?* Notice how consumed your attention tends to be with others' needs or feelings. Balance this by offering generous servings of loving attentiveness and quality service to your own previously hidden or forbidden feelings, needs, and desires.

e3: *When will I feel fulfilled?* Notice how habitually your attention hurdles over feelings and toward an ever-moving goal. Balance this by being patiently and compassionately curious about what you are feeling. Recognize that the feelings you believe are in your way are actually the stepstones into personal fulfillment.

e4: *How am I blessed?* Notice how habitually your attention dwells on what is missing. Balance this by identifying and describing to others what is blessed, bountiful, and beautiful about your life today.

e5: *What am I sharing?* Notice how often your attention goes to self-conservation and fending off intrusion. Balance this by making a consistent, concerted practice of volunteering—especially when it comes to sharing your feelings, energy, or engaged presence.

e6: *What do I hope for?* Notice how often your attention goes selectively toward negative information while tending to doubt or discount what is positive or hopeful. Balance this by making a practice of entertaining best-case scenarios and positive outcomes for all the future storylines you imagine.

e7: *When might I love and live wholeheartedly?* Notice how regularly your attention is fragmented as you mentally plan for future pleasure while running from present pain. Balance this by anchoring your awareness in your heart. Chances are you'll find unprocessed heartache there. Making time to embrace your difficult feelings enables you to stop settling for superficial, short-term gratification and allows you to experience the depths of real self-love.

e8: *How often am I truly receptive to others?* Notice how often your attention goes toward resisting others and your environment in order to maintain your personal autonomy and sense of control. Practice balancing this by intentionally releasing your grip and letting others be in charge, whether at home or work. Experience what it's like when you consent to softening, relaxing, and going along with others' wants, needs, or agendas.

e9: *Am I listening attentively?* Notice how readily your attention gets distracted or diverted from whatever you are doing, feeling, or thinking. Balance this by regularly checking in with yourself. Treat yourself as you would a good friend. Ask yourself how you're doing and what you are thinking or feeling. Then listen attentively. As important as it is to matter to others, it is so much more important to matter to yourself.

Reflect: What did you notice about your habit of attention? Enlist the Inner Observer (Practice 3) here and add the Mystical Awe (Practice 6) if you need additional support in breaking free of the attentional patterns of your type.

For where your treasure is, there your heart will be also.

—Matthew 6:21

Deserving Abundance

No matter how qualified or deserving we are, we will never reach a better life until we can imagine it for ourselves and allow ourselves to have it.

—Richard Bach, author of *Illusions*

Each Ennea-type tends to cut itself off from life's goodness, abundance, and bounty in particular ways. At the end of the day, it is vital to remember that peace, joy, and love are everyone's divine birthright, including our own.

We have a list of things we deem are never going to happen for us, not possible for us, or available only to select others, informed by our type. When we set that list aside and say "Yes" and "Now" to the infinite wellspring of divine abundance that is *already* present, we do so not as a matter of striving but as an act of spiritual openness, surrender, and faith. Gratitude (Practice 5) and Affirmative Prayer (Practice 9) can both be particularly helpful here.

The personality tends to construct rigid ideas about the form we think life's bounty is supposed to take. The soul knows the riches of Spirit are ever-present within us, beneath us, above us, behind us, and before us, in perfection. In truth, we live and move and have our being in Spirit's abundance.

Following are nine ways to activate our faith-lens and expand the horizon of blessing we can perceive and receive, remembering that as we receive, we do so not just for ourselves; in the receiving, we are given what we need to show up in our highest and fullest every moment of every day, for the good of *all*.

As you read this activation, see if you can sense your heart and body. Let your entire being soften into the possibility that the following statements of worthiness are indeed profoundly true of and for you. Cease trying to cultivate or earn what is freely available, and simply set your intention to permit yourself to receive it.

Activation by Type

e1: I deserve deep peace. I gently step outside my self-made prison of unforgiveness and cease the inner violence of warring with what was and what is.

e2: I deserve abundant love. I resist insistently prioritizing others' needs before my own.

e3: I deserve absolute grace. I restrain myself from incessant productivity and rest from striving to earn my worth.

e4: I deserve unconditional belonging without conformity. I show up honestly in all my relationships and take my rightful place in the diverse array of life.

e5: I deserve faith and confidence in having enough to show up and share of my time, talent, and resources. I open my heart to feeling how showing up with others can restore rather than deplete me.

e6: I deserve warmth and support. Care need not be steady to be real. I let myself trust in others' kindnesses without doubting or deflecting.

e7: I deserve satisfaction. I let myself fully relish who I am, where I am, and all that I already possess in the here and now, including what I see as the challenges of this moment.

e8: I deserve nurturing. I remove my armor and willingly open myself to receiving heartfelt care in ways that may feel threatening and make me feel vulnerable, appreciating that *authentic* strength bears the transformational beams of love.

e9: I deserve to shine. I relinquish judgment of myself or others around taking up space. I resist shrinking, and let myself be the center of attention more often—others' attention, but also my own!

Reflect: How does it feel to read these statements—your type's or others'? To what extent were you able to take in the abundance proposition for your type?

Prosperity is a way of living and thinking, and not just money or things.

—Eric Butterworth, *Spiritual Economics*

Self-Care

*I found in my research that the biggest reason people aren't
more self-compassionate is that they are afraid they'll become
self-indulgent. They believe self-criticism is what keeps them
in line. Most people have gotten it wrong because our
culture says being hard on yourself is the way to be.*

—Kristin Neff

Certainly, we may have seen others go the way of hedonism, addiction, and self-indulgence in a manner that hurts not only themselves but others around them. So, how can you best tell the difference between self-indulgence and self-care? One of the key components I've seen in my pastoral care work as well as in my consulting work supporting family and professional caregivers is that authentic self-care is restorative and life-giving. When we experience it, we are inclined to show up with *more* presence and compassion in our lives for ourselves and others. The following activation offers self-care practices recommended for each type, which might seem unacceptable or indulgent to that type at first glance but can be a healing salve based on our type's tendencies to steer us away from what we truly need.

Activation by Type

e1: Today, I practice taking myself and others less seriously. I bring a sense of perspective, lightness, and good humor to my day.

e2: Today, I practice self-affirmation by making space to honor my more challenging emotions. I accept that it's okay for me to not feel okay.

e3: Today, I practice self-care by focusing on recreation and enjoyment rather than discipline and self-improvement.

e4: Today, I cherish myself by being self-starting and disciplined, rather than indulging my moods in a way that is self-defeating.

e5: Today, I honor my needs for connection by initiating physical or emotional contact with a friend or loved one.

e6: Today, I practice gratitude for my physical body, whatever its present condition. I visualize myself as strong and grounded.

e7: Today, I practice savoring every morsel and every moment, gently bringing my attention back to the present whenever I find it has strayed.

e8: Today, I remember to pause before adding more to my plate. I discern which actions truly support my highest dreams and core values.

e9: Today, I make healthful choices that energize me—physically, emotionally, and mentally!

Reflect: Did you find it challenging to engage the self-care practice for your type? What practices from other types did you find attractive or helpful? Elaborate.

Can you feel the rush? Listen quietly. It's there. It's the
sound of a life and spirit being set free. God, help me set
myself free from ridiculous and unnecessary expectations.

—Melody Beattie

Relationship Trances

A soul connection is a resonance between two people who respond to the essential beauty of each other's individual natures, behind their facades, and who connect on this deeper level. This kind of mutual recognition provides the catalyst for a potent alchemy. It is a sacred alliance whose purpose is to help both partners discover and realize their deepest potentials. . . . A soul connection not only inspires us to expand, but also forces us to confront whatever stands in the way of that expansion.

—John Welwood, *Love and Awakening*

The Enneagram is a powerful tool for self-awareness—a prerequisite for fulfilling relationships. Learning the Enneagram helps us to live into our fullness and magnificence, in part, by describing the ways we get trapped in the *trance of type*. Recognizing that we're in a trance is a starting point for waking up. We begin to see how our type structure might be sabotaging true intimacy and soulful connection. Consider engaging the Namasté practice (Practice 7) in tandem with your type's activation.

Activation by Type

e1: When in the trance of type, you tend to think criticizing your loved ones is the best way to improve your relationships. However, doing so typically creates a fiercely unaccepting (and thus unsafe) relational space that is toxic to genuine intimacy. Do your best to welcome intimacy and trust by affirming with sincerity what's good in your loved ones instead. Practice this in your unspoken thoughts as well as by voicing your appreciation directly.

e2: When in the trance of type, you tend to cultivate dependency in others as protection against rejection. After all, if they need you, how could they leave you? This often leaves you resentful, exhausted, and unavailable for the closeness and reciprocity you desire. Be willing to risk rejection to experience authentic relationships of mutual respect, generosity, and care.

e3: When in the trance of type, you tend to get lost in the role you play—whether as a partner, parent, or friend. Even if others love and admire your role, you don't end up really feeling loved for who you are. The only way to know your true belovedness is to mindfully catch yourself in the act as often as you can and willingly stop performing.

e4: When in the trance of type, you tend to become confused about what is real. Too often, your romanticized ideals feel more intense and deeper (and thus more real) than the actual people and events happening right in front of you. True authenticity invites you to wake up from your reverie. Only then will you find the magic you've been missing—in what at first feels mundane.

e5: When in the trance of type, you habitually disconnect from your feelings in real time, which can come across as cold or uncaring to those you love. People can't always tell how sensitive you are. Sometimes beneath that cold exterior you are feeling rejected or hurt. Connect more deeply with others by checking in with yourself to identify what you are truly feeling. Step out of your comfort zone by opening up to your loved ones about feelings you've compartmentalized and stuffed deep down inside. Experiment with trust as a gateway to truly satisfying interactions.

e6: When in the trance of type, you can sometimes poke and test others too often, even unconsciously. Constantly testing others' loyalty or affection can wear them down. You end up eroding the very solidity you are trying to obtain. While you're never going to stop asking for confirmation or testing through trials, see if you can simply do this less often and assume others' good intentions and steadiness of heart more often.

e7: When in the trance of type, you tend to be highly distractible, which can feel dismissive and disrespectful to others. With those who matter, practice giving them your undivided attention. Listen not just with your head but also with your heart so you can actually feel what might be going on for them. Ultimately, you'll find that being more present with both mind and heart isn't just a gift to the other person; it makes the interaction much more amazing for you as well.

e8: When in the trance of type, you tend to be highly individualistic, making and changing plans on the fly, unthinkingly leaving those you care about out of the loop. Strategically withholding information for fear of being controlled is a way you try to maintain power and autonomy over your situation. While it might feel threatening at first, choosing to let loved ones in on your activities and being receptive to feedback can help you to cocreate a life much bigger and better than any you had dreamt of on your own.

e9: When in the trance of type, you tend to merge with others or do your best to blend in to belong, letting your individual identity fade into the background of the life you share with others, whether at home or work. However, self-abandonment takes its toll and, over time, you completely check out of the relationship. Be willing to check *in* with yourself on a routine basis by patiently yet persistently asking yourself: *What are* my *true wants, feelings, and opinions?*

Reflect: How did the way you think of and relate to others change as you engaged this activation? Did you pair this with Namasté (Practice 7)? Can you better perceive the wholeness and holiness of others as well as yourself?

> *Every relationship has a spiritual purpose that helps us grow*
> *and become stronger. Sometimes, our most challenging*
> *relationships bring the greatest personal blessings. From*
> *them we learn about forgiveness, patience, and other virtues.*

—Doreen Virtue, American author

Sacred Receiving

May you experience each day as a sacred
gift woven around the heart of wonder.

—John O'Donohue, *Eternal Echoes*

This activation is about letting life and letting *yourself* be enough—and about finding rest and a sense of sufficiency in the sacred. The following activation is most powerfully read, whether quietly or aloud, as "I" statements.

Here, we consider approaching our days with less of a "sweating and a striving" and more of a "receiving and allowing" attitude. Here, we might entertain worrying less about the outer world and finding more sanctuary in our inner lives. Here, we might find rest in the God of our own understanding.

Granted, for some of us, resting can be harder than working. Asking for help can feel more humiliating than suffering alone. Receiving can feel more conflictual than giving. Perhaps this is a time to shift that. Perhaps this is a time to welcome a more abundant, grace-filled way of being in the world.

Activation by Type

e1: I relinquish a sense of burden and invite a state of grace.

e2: I refuse to be defined by whether my decisions please others.

e3: I participate in activities for their own sake—for my soul's sake.

e4: I elevate my experience by bringing mindfulness to everyday tasks.

e5: I share sacred relationship space, connecting more openly with others.

e6: I am inextricably tethered to an invisible, invincible stronghold.

e7: I surrender the thought, *What's next?* and faithfully embrace what is right here, right now.

e8: I soften toward the world around me, seeing it through childlike eyes.

e9: I surrender to my passions by engaging my life more zestfully—with mind, heart, body, and spirit!

Reflect: What might it mean for you to rest here, now, in omnipresent Love and welcome a sense of the sacred?

> *Through your love*
> *existence and nonexistence merge.*
> *All opposites unite.*
> *All that is profane*
> *becomes sacred again.*
> —Rumi

Transforming Type Tendencies

Without struggle, no progress and no result.
Every breaking of habit produces a change in the machine.

—Gurdjieff

As a spiritual teacher, George Ivanovich Gurdjieff taught that humans are but machines and that, for the most part, we operate on autopilot, sleepwalking through life. Recent psychological studies have shown that when people make choices that include a default option, they tend to select that option. Too often, we resort to Ennea-type behaviors automatically and lose sight of the fuller spectrum of possibilities available to us. The following activation reminds us that our type has certain default attitudes and behaviors and when we are not attentive and making conscious choices, we will automatically resort to well-worn patterns. Keep in mind: this activation is not about making any of the type defaults wrong; rather, it is about giving us conscious choice.

Activation by Type

e1: You tend to think personal growth is best achieved through hard work, discipline, and self-regulation. Being overly self-controlled, however, can stifle your transformation. Try surrendering control in more and more instances—not as a gesture of defeat but as a practice of faith—and then see what unfolds.

e2: You tend to believe your lovability lies in being of service to the special people in your life. Being overly available and attentive to others' needs, however, means you lose bandwidth to even notice, much less respond, to your own. Be willing to be less "on call" for others so you can bring your tremendous gifts of cheerleading and counseling to yourself. Take your own good advice today!

e3: You tend to believe your value hinges on being the best in all categories of life in which you care to compete. In your haste to win or get ahead, however, you can lose contact with something essential within yourself. Consider where you're willing to be last in order to put your authentic self first.

e4: You tend to believe your importance lies in the ways you are unique. This causes you to over-identify with those parts of you that seem to not belong. You focus your suffering on this apparent "not belonging," but what if your true suffering comes from the fear of fitting in? Radical healing happens when you embrace traits in you that seem common or shared with others.

e5: You tend to believe that enlightenment can only happen once you figure it all out. Life, however, is not a problem to be solved, but a reality to be lived. All the grandest ideas in the world will not offer you the inner knowing that is irrefutable in the moments you fully release researching or observing life in favor of directly feeling and sensing it.

e6: You tend to believe your faith needs to be 100 percent certain to be valid. But the ground of your transformation lies in your inner capacity to trust that what you know for now is more than enough. As you identify more and more with this part of you that remains steadfast amid the changing landscape of life, you begin to sense the infinite and eternal embedded in what appears finite and mortal.

e7: You tend to believe your happiness is in the next new thing, person, or activity. The issue with this is not that your good never comes but, rather, that you are not here to receive it. Your best life is like a package you must be home to sign for and that includes items you never ordered. Spiritual freedom begins when you trust life enough to accept this entire package anyway.

e8: You tend to believe you can power your way through any challenge. Spiritual unfoldment, however, demands softness rather than hardness. Rather than increase your intensity, drop into the most tender parts of your heart and open to what feels weakest or most debilitating. Discover what it's like to be *willing* rather than *willful*.

e9: You tend to believe that the less disturbed you feel, the more peaceful the world will become. But the path to inner and outer unity and harmony depends on your capacity to embrace conflict and differences, not only in others but, significantly, within yourself. The paradox for you is that universal peace is achieved through first embracing what is personal to you and inviting your distinctiveness to color the larger fabric of life.

Reflect: What new perspectives or choices opened to you because of practicing your type's activation?

> *Until you make the unconscious conscious,*
> *it will direct your life and you will call it fate.*

—Carl Jung, Swiss psychiatrist and psychotherapist

Healing Our Wounds

Imagine that you have a thorn in your arm that directly touches a nerve. When the thorn is touched, it's very painful. Because it hurts so much, the thorn is a serious problem. It's difficult to sleep because you roll over on it. It's hard to get close to people because they might touch it. It makes your daily life very difficult. You can't even go for a walk in the woods because you might brush the thorn against the branches. This thorn is a constant source of disturbance, and to solve the problem you only have two choices. The first choice is to look at your situation and decide that since it's so disturbing when things touch the thorn, you need to make sure nothing touches it. The second choice is to decide that since it's so disturbing when things touch the thorn, you need to take it out.

—Michael A. Singer, *The Untethered Soul*

Too often, we make the first choice Michael Singer refers to in this passage; then we devote our lives to making sure nothing and no one gets near our thorn. Even if we succeed in protecting that wounded part of ourselves, when everything is said and done, our wounded self is dictating every aspect of our lives.

The following activation invites you to make the second choice—expose your wounds, type-based and otherwise, to light and love for transformation and healing.

Activation by Type

e1: Even the slightest criticism can sometimes cut you to your core because it seems to affirm a foundational fear of yours: *There is something wrong with me.* Can you let yourself feel your hurt without needing to make the other person bad or wrong? Can you widen your focus to assess more objectively what is or is not valid about the critique? Can you enlarge your self-love to make sure it is not based on the unattainable ideal of showing up perfectly?

e2: Lack of appreciation by a special somebody can render you all kinds of furious. When lit up, you often use that fire to hustle even more for approval or recognition. Can you instead use this opportunity to tenderly inquire into your own unmet needs? Can you admit to what extent you may have prioritized helping another in hopes of gaining that person's esteem or acknowledgment at your own expense? Can you now bring the same level of devotion to tending to your own sense of worth and wellbeing?

e3: Even a small failure can feel so untenable that you repaint it as a success. Can you see what happens if you trust that the rising and falling of your outer success is less about you personally and perhaps simply the movement of life? Can you rest in the flow of life and feel it carry you to places you never planned? Can you receive this blessing as an ongoing gift of grace, without needing to believe that, through your hard efforts, you have especially earned it?

e4: Not having your sense of uniqueness mirrored back can feel tragic. It can bring up a sense of shame that you're too ordinary to be noticed or to be worthy of special attention or mention. You tend to believe what you're feeling is true. Can you test this by dropping your attention beneath the feeling? Can you sense a solidity within you that has always been whole? Can you see how there is an authentic core within you that does not need to be seen by others to feel valid or real?

e5: Being questioned regarding your competency can bring up some of your darkest emotions and trigger your terror of being useless or helpless. Chances are all it took was someone asking a sincere question. Then you were off and running, gathering mental data in defense of your actions or decisions. What if you resisted the need to prove what (or how much) you know? What if you also released scorn or judgment around others who don't have the same capacity or desire to think things through as thoroughly as you typically do?

e6: Your efforts to provide yourself and those you love with adequate security, support, and/or guidance can become all consuming. Preparing doggedly for the worst can keep you from experiencing the best that life has to offer now. Can you give yourself a break from first attempting to make only the safest, most prudent plans and then beating yourself up if you missed a detail or neglected to consider every single contingency?

e7: The idea of being trapped and in pain is terrifying. Too often, however, in your frenetic efforts to run from feelings of pain or limitation, you end up causing suffering for yourself and those you love. When you compulsively run toward the next new idea or indulgence, you can tend to break trust, spend beyond your means, or even get into ethical or legal trouble. Can you see how your perpetual escapism compounds your pain and becomes its own kind of prison?

e8: Your fear of being harmed or controlled can result in you inadvertently dominating or controlling others. You often try to guard your own autonomy or personal space, but the power and speed with which you instinctively react can cause damage you never intended. Can you practice intercepting your reactivity by pausing to consider a perspective that doesn't automatically assume others are against you? Are you willing to consider that others who have caused you harm didn't bear ill intent?

e9: Your inner tale of being invisible is a self-fulfilling prophecy. You check out (and sometimes literally fall asleep) so you don't have to face the desolation of being left out. You strive to blend in but then balk (yet again) at being over-looked or forgotten. Can you catch yourself self-censoring an idea or opinion that might stand out? Can you err on the side of taking what you consider to be too much time or space because throughout your life you most certainly have claimed too little?

Reflect: How much time and energy have you used to prevent life from getting near any of your wounds? Were you able and willing to practice your type's activation?

It is easier to put on a pair of shoes than to wrap the earth in leather.

—Chögyam Trungpa, Tibetan Buddhist teacher

The wound is the place where the light enters you.

—Rumi

Defense Mechanisms

The defenses are part and parcel of our type structure. Although we are not limited to just one defense mechanism—we can use any of them— one of them is more closely associated with our type. In fact, the defense mechanism appropriates the strength of our type and diverts this capacity to keep us safe, or at least to keep our ego intact.

—Peter O'Hanrahan, Core faculty of The Narrative Enneagram

As we endeavor to embrace our wholeness, our type-based psychological defenses operate to defend and uphold our type structures and thereby preserve who we *think* we are. As we embark on the soul's journey of transformation, our defense mechanisms go on alert.

Becoming aware of these defenses as they arise and sensing how they feel in our bodies can support us in loosening their grip on our personas. Rather than wage war with our defenses, we can approach them with compassionate curiosity, acknowledging how hard they try to protect our sense of self.

Over time and with gentle attention, our defensiveness transforms, offering our souls greater space and freedom of expression.

Activation by Type

e1: Notice how often you activate the defense mechanism of *reaction formation* to quash any thoughts, feelings, or behaviors you deem bad or unacceptable by reflexively responding in a manner that is the exact opposite of your authentic responses. For instance, perhaps you have behaved with rigid politeness because you were quite irritated with someone. Constantly towing the narrow moral line in this way can temporarily quiet your inner critic, but it only breeds deeper resentment given the extraordinary self-control required for your herculean efforts to improve the world. When you give yourself permission to own what feels darkest about you and then consciously choose how to behave, you make the world a better place.

e2: Notice how you use the defense mechanism of *repression* to keep feelings or needs that don't fit your self-concept as a giving and generous person far from your line of sight. While repression operates unconsciously, its results are often detectable in your words and actions. It might show up blatantly, such as in an unexpected burst of anger. It might also express itself more covertly in the ways you subtly manipulate, guilt, or seduce someone into giving you what you want or need. There is great relief in coming clean about what you desire, need, or are struggling through. Directly asking for support is a courageous act of self-love.

e3: Notice how you use the defense mechanism of *identification* to incorporate the characteristics of those you admire into your sense of self. You do this unconsciously, enacting qualities you value while hiding who you actually are because, deep down, you believe that just being you is simply not good enough. You are convinced you must turn yourself into someone of value—as seen through others' eyes. One clue this is happening is that you feel empty inside. What is missing for your ultimate fulfillment is the true you!

e4: Notice how often you use the defense mechanism of *introjection* to protect your sense of self, tending to block positive data while internalizing others' negative feedback as your own judgment. Instead of directly experiencing the pain of someone else hurting you, you neutralize the impact by experiencing it as if it is self-inflicted, which somehow feels more manageable. Recognize that your mind is habituated toward thinking less of yourself. Knowing this, recognize that your authentic self is likely far more amazing than you're admitting. Cherish yourself enough to bring awareness to your own beauty and wholeness.

e5: Notice how you use the defense mechanism of *isolation*—retreating into your mind, cutting yourself off from feelings, and compartmentalizing different areas of your life to help you avoid a sense of overwhelm or depletion. You may also isolate yourself physically or compartmentalize different social groups. While you certainly do need some solitude and separation, make a conscious effort to recognize the point at which your physical, emotional, or mental isolation is not actually nourishing you but rather leaving you feeling useless or lonely. Reach out to others to make meaningful connections and to offer your active participation.

e6: Notice how you use the defense mechanism of *projection*, unconsciously attributing your own unacceptable qualities, motives, or behaviors to others. This applies to even positive qualities, such as good-heartedness, intelligence, or strength. While you might default to projection to reduce anxiety in situations that feel ambiguous, uncertain, or otherwise dangerous, it can actually raise your anxiety level and cause you to live in an imagined reality. Checking in with yourself and bravely doing a reality check with others about your negative projections will help you to be in authentic relationship with them—and with what is actually going on for both of you. But bravery also means checking in to see if you're deflecting sincere compliments that reflect strengths you've been reluctant to recognize in yourself. By recognizing when you are projecting, you are empowered to embrace disowned parts of yourself (positive as well as negative) and to more clearly perceive the situation at hand.

e7: Notice when you resort to the defense mechanism of *rationalizing*—namely, positively reframing your behavior to sidestep difficult feelings or avoid taking personal responsibility. You often justify your rationalization on the basis that it protects others from pain or upset; if you're honest, however, it is because you fear that their upset will cause *you* pain. While it might feel backward, owning up to your true motivations and making space for negative feelings (yours as well as others) goes further than any forced positivity does toward achieving a happier outcome.

e8: Notice when you are maintaining your inner sense of being powerful by using the psychological defense mechanism of *denial* to reject the existence or seriousness of anything that feels unacceptable to you (especially things that bring up anxiety, sadness, or vulnerabilities). Your ability to ignore pain and power through hard times can often serve to weaken rather than strengthen you. Whether the issue is emotional, physical, or material, acknowledging and accepting the condition is the beginning of healing from it.

e9: Notice how you fall back on the defense mechanism of *narcotization*—going on autopilot when you feel pressured and overwhelmed or discounted and overlooked. If you're willing to defy the pull toward sleepwalking through your day (or literally falling asleep) and opt to directly address irritating stressors, you avoid prolonging the pain and the risk of slipping into the darkness of an unlived life. *Bring your truth to light!*

Reflect: Often, transformation occurs as soon as we bring conscious awareness to what was previously an unconscious reaction on the part of the personality. What happened for you as you recognized your defense mechanism in play?

> *If you begin to understand what you are without trying to*
> *change it, then what you are undergoes a transformation.*

—Jiddu Krishnamurti, Indian philosopher and orator

The Lives We Create

Make each day your masterpiece.

—John Wooden, American basketball coach

The following activation is about having a bit of fun and allowing ourselves space to think playfully and creatively about our lives. Try these out and, most of all, let yourself play! This is not about formally being artists. It's about recognizing we are already part of the natural creative process of life. Give yourself permission to be messy and silly!

Activation by Type

e1: If your entire week was a blank canvas, what activities would you paint to represent joy, delight, or spontaneity?

e2: If you created something for yourself alone, what would it be?

e3: If you could draw a face that accurately portrays what you truly feel today, what image would you see?

e4: Spend five to ten minutes today imagining yourself in the here and now with every quality you think you've been missing. What would it feel like to be this very person?

e5: If you wrote an autobiography highlighting your life, how many different activities would you write about? How many involve thinking or researching? If you were to add a new activity you haven't yet done but hope to do, what would it be?

e6: Spend five to ten minutes today visualizing yourself in a world where everything turns out great. What are you doing? Use as many of your senses as possible in this exercise!

e7: Take five to ten minutes to consider the landscape of your heart. Look closely. What does it look like? What feelings come up for you as you imagine this scene?

e8: If you built a vacation home for your inner child, what would your home include and why?

e9: If you sang a ballad of your life, who would be the main character? What would be the key themes of your song?

Reflect: What, if anything, surprised you about this exercise? Was it easy or challenging to give yourself artistic license and not worry about finding a "right" way to respond to your type's activation?

> *Don't be satisfied with stories, how things have*
> *gone with others. Unfold your own myth.*
>
> —Rumi

Rigorous Honesty in Healing

You cannot heal what you do not first acknowledge.

—Richard Rohr, *Breathing Underwater*

Transformation requires rigorous self-honesty. First, we must admit to our vices and the ways we are showing up from our own woundedness and sense of separation. Second, rather than trying to put the pieces together ourselves, we invite the light of Spirit to illumine our hearts and pave our way. It's vital to have faith in the process, even when things seem to be going worse for a while, trusting that if we've sincerely opened ourselves to Spirit, grace is healing and transforming our consciousness and, through that, our lives.

The following activation highlights areas of our humanity that tend to be obscured depending on our type.

Activation by Type

e1: When you openly admit you are angry and then drop beneath to the hurt inside you, true healing can happen. Rather than ask, *What did so-and-so do wrong?* ask *What need of mine wasn't being met when that happened?* and *How might I skillfully approach getting my need met without having to make anyone bad or wrong?*

e2: When you openly admit to being too prideful to acknowledge your own needs—whether they be your needs for assurance or guidance or even hands-on assistance—true healing can happen. Rather than maintain inequality in relationships to assure others depend on you but you don't depend on them, see where you can develop relationships of greater mutuality and shared respect.

e3: When you openly admit to being inauthentic—because you cover up your true feelings and needs to play the part or get the job done—true healing can happen. First, take time to recognize what is true for you. Then, rather than putting on the face you think will get the best response from everyone else, take the chance of letting at least a few select others in, even and especially if you are feeling ashamed about this part of yourself.

e4: When you openly admit to being envious of others' happiness, true healing can happen. Happiness is not about what others have that you don't have. Rather, true joy comes from fully embracing, rather than shaming, all parts of you. The gifts of your life are unique and no one else's good can keep you from your own.

e5: When you openly admit to your fear of rejection, true healing can begin. You realize there are times you are standoffish—behaving as if you don't need someone or don't want to do something when you actually do. Recognize that, deep down, you fear how incompetent and overwhelmed you feel trying to meet not only your needs but others' needs, expectations, and demands in all your interactions. Take a moment to honor the importance of just showing up; you don't have to take on *everything*, just come to the interaction with openness, responsiveness, and patience toward others and yourself.

e6: When you openly admit to letting anxiety overtake you, true healing can happen. Take charge by taking three deep breaths and becoming aware of your physical body, noticing your hands and feet. Fear is strengthened by your attention to the future. By anchoring yourself in the sensations of your body, you ground yourself in the present moment, where your tremendous courage and strength reside.

e7: When you openly admit to your fear of being internally barren and bereft of joy, true healing can happen. Letting go of thinking about the next or the new; to fill that inner sense of emptiness is, for you, the best chance for finding true renewal. Committing to the present moment is one of the most rewarding things you can do. Give yourself the gift of cultivating a lifelong friendship, through good times and hard times, with the here and now.

e8: When you openly admit to how much you vigorously defend against vulnerability, true healing can happen. Weaker muscles are strengthened by exercise and wounds heal more fully when exposed to light. Shielding parts of yourself you fear might be used against you is one way your resistance to ever being harmed or betrayed drives you to live in a harsher reality than you need to. While not everyone has earned the right to your trust, consider being more open with those who have.

e9: When you can openly admit to the terror of feeling insignificant, true healing can happen. Engaging your fear and boldly showing up anyway will do more for your wellbeing than escape through alternately overworking or numbing out. In this drama called life, while you resist taking the stage and thereby standing out, the truth is no one can effectively *stand in* for you. You are much needed and irreplaceable.

Reflect: What have you come to openly admit not only to yourself but to the God of your understanding? How has that admission impacted your life?

> *In failing to confess, Lord, I would only hide*
> *You from myself, not myself from You.*
>
> —Saint Augustine of Hippo

Your Inner Dynamism

*Here is the main thing: the lines are the basic building blocks
of the Enneagram, not the points. An Enneagram line is an
archetype, a collection of themes, like a novel or a life. These
themes are meant to be engaged, participated in, and wrestled with.*

—Michael J. Goldberg, author of *The 9 Ways of Working*

The Enneagram is a dynamic (aka psychodynamic) system. If you look at the Enneagram symbol, you will notice that each number around the circle has two inner lines attached to it. For example, the 6 has one line to 3 and another to 9. The 2 has one line to 8 and another to 4, and so on for all the types.

As we move along the lines within the Enneagram symbol, our personality goes through a significant, if only temporary, change. At the points where the lines radiating from our core type end, we experience a very different point of view and style of behavior.

Decades ago, it was taught that when we move along the inner lines of the Enneagram in the following direction (3 to 9, 9 to 6, and 6 to 3; 1 to 4, 4 to 2, 2 to 8, 8 to 5, 5 to 7, and 7 to 1), we are invariably on a path of *disintegration* and when we move along the inner lines in the opposite direction (3 to 6, 6 to 9, 9 to 3; 1 to 7, 7 to 5, 5 to 8, 8 to 2, 2 to 4, 4 to 1) we are invariably moving along a path of *integration* toward wholeness. However, in the last decade or so, Enneagram teachers have come to more correctly and fully understand that it is not quite that simple. In reality, we can go to either the low or the high side of either of these points on the Enneagram—that is to say, we can express the less healthy or the healthier qualities of both points along our lines.

In the direction historically called our *line of disintegration* lies our *stress point* (aka *resource point*[6]). We tend to go this direction by default when we are under significant stress. For example, as a Type 3, I used to work doggedly, completely unaware of any of my feelings, what time it might be, and whether my body needed anything like food or rest. Then come Friday evening, when others might be ready for an outing, I would just conk out early and sleep through to the next morning.

I also had cycles of burnout in which I would numb out with an entire television series, or food binge, or both. Basically, without recognizing it at the time, I was going to the low side of my resource point, point 9—not intentionally resting but rather numbing, withdrawing, and checking out at point 9. Notably, it can be very uncomfortable to stay at our resource point, especially when we've dropped into it by default rather than intentionally going there to tap into the higher qualities of that point.

In the other direction (along what is historically called our *line of integration*) lies our *heart point* (sometimes called the *security point*). When we travel toward our heart point, we come to inhabit a set of qualities considered to be very valuable for our inner growth and transformation. This point holds a key to many of our *shadow qualities*—namely, qualities we have repressed that are essential to our wholeness. We tend to naturally go to this point when we're feeling secure. This point tends to embody qualities that our type judges, censors, and forbids. This is why it can be helpful to have one-on-one or community support in working with the Enneagram. We often reject the very qualities we most need. As someone who leads with point 3, moving toward point 6 energy challenges my propensity to go about life alone just so I can go faster. Yet, in this way, it offers me one of the gifts I have most dearly sought throughout my life—the gift of authentic connection and community.

As you reflect on the following activation, keep in mind that it is not intended to provide an exhaustive description of what it means to touch on the higher qualities of your type's connecting points. This is merely an invitation to try out certain qualities of being that relate to, but differ from those more central to your type.

Activation by Type

e1: Consciously tapping into the energies of your connecting points of 7 and 4, experience the expansiveness of thinking skyward as well as the deepening that comes from allowing the colorful array of your actual feelings. These inner movements can help you show up from a richer, more full-bodied place where life isn't so much about the minutia, and nothing is starkly black and white.

e2: Consciously tapping into the energies of your connecting points of 4 and 8, delve below surface emotions to your deeper, sometimes darker, motivations while experiencing the steadiness that comes from grounding in your body. These inner movements can help you charge toward what you truly want and need with greater boldness and conviction.

e3: Consciously tapping into the energies of your connecting points of 6 and 9, bring a more considered approach and a more collaborative spirit to your actions while intentionally slowing down enough to feel the splendor of the journey and not just the destination. These inner movements can help you receive the joy of simply existing as well as the tremendous gift of feeling genuine care and connection with others.

e4: Consciously tapping into the energies of your connecting points of 1 and 2, apply self-control to your restless energy and experience the sense of belonging that can come from expressing warmth, generosity, and curiosity toward others. These inner movements can help you escape the slippery slope of moody withdrawal, which only leads to more shame, suffering, and loneliness.

e5: Consciously tapping into the energies of your connecting points of 8 and 7, practice standing your ground and taking concrete action on your ideas even while holding hands with your imaginative childlike energy. These inner movements can help you balance your heady inwardness with a more energized, enthusiastic, and embodied worldliness.

e6: Consciously tapping into the energies of your connecting points of 9 and 3, find the stillness within your mental storm and then, with the clarity that arises from your inner peace, come to a place of resolution. These inner movements can help you to transform paralyzing doubt or constant second guessing into calm, faithful, and steadfast action.

e7: Consciously tapping into the energies of your connecting points of 5 and 1, slow down, steady your pace, and apply the discipline it takes to envision and plan with greater depth and detail. These inner movements can help you relinquish lifelong self-sabotage and gain the sweet satisfaction of completing your goals and realizing your wildest dreams.

e8: Consciously tapping into the energies of your connecting points of 2 and 5, get in contact with your emotional vulnerability and practice exercising more cool-headed caution before acting. These inner movements can help you lead more with your mind and heart (and not just your gut), helping you bring greater effectiveness and big heartedness to all that you say and do.

e9: Consciously tapping into the energies of your connecting points of 3 and 6, focus your energy and organize your thoughts as you edge out of your comfort zone of blissful fantasies and idealizations. These inner movements can help you experience just enough of a destabilizing jolt to mobilize effective and efficient action on your personal real-world goals.

Reflect: We can have some of the strongest resistance and most negative judgments about the points along our type's moving lines. Often, this is because the qualities embodied by the lower-health expressions of that point contradict the idealized self for our type. For instance, as a Three, I have historically been most judgmental of the low side of point 9,[7] which is laziness. Moving toward wholeness has been about recognizing that the Three's tendency to overvalue work and productivity resulted in my condemning as "lazy" my very legitimate needs for rest and enjoyment of life.

> *To transform . . . we must . . . allow our defenses to crack open and break down—and consciously integrate our disowned feelings, blind spots, and Shadow traits so that we can shake off the limiting outer shell of our personality and grow into all that we are meant to be.*

—Beatrice Chestnut, *The Complete Enneagram*

New Paradigms

*I knew that to accomplish my goal I would need to stay
present with my discomfort and my fear of the unknown
rather than retreat to the false safety of familiar ground.*

—Debbie Ford, *The Secret of the Shadow*

Transformation requires that we be willing to do more than change our behaviors. It demands a shift in how we view our world and our relationship to it. In this sense, we are asked to leave the familiar territory of our historical life paradigms and venture into ideas that might seem quite foreign and even dangerous to entertain. This activation is for you to consider as you enter new terrain, where your old map of the world and how life works might no longer be useful.

Activation by Type

e1: Your lofty ideals are but idols that you worship instead of Truth. Lowering your standards to render them more "reasonable" doesn't fix the foundational problem that standards are all relative to one point of view, by which you judge one thing as higher or lower, better or worse, nobler or baser. What if you neither raised nor lowered your standards but let them go altogether? What if, without a measuring stick, you could experience the full reality of something's height directly? What if you applied this practice to encountering people and not just things?

e2: You cannot force-feed others to fill your own hunger for love. This cultivates dependencies, leaving both of you caught in a loop of perpetual indebtedness. You cannot buy self-esteem with this counterfeit currency. What would happen if you neglected others' needs for a time and sat alone within the chamber of your own heart and treasured your worth with your own shiny attentiveness? What if your heart ate all of this up?

e3: Your tendency to believe that *everything is up to me* is the death of pure creativity. It separates you from the flow of the universe. From there, life can only be lonely and hard. So, you develop a strong, competitive, fighting spirit and lack of restraint. What would happen, however, if you stilled yourself, if only for minutes between those hours of intense striving? Would you lose your flow—or would you finally find your true self within it?

e4: True authenticity involves accepting the ordinary—rather than enhancing it. When you attune to the subtleties of your heart's dance, you'll notice you sometimes take what is only slightly difficult and spin it until it feels unmanageable. Feeling powerless and out of control, you'll then look for equanimity outside yourself. What if you stopped dramatically exiting yourself to look for what feels missing and realized instead that what feels missing is already in you? What if there is a perfect and beautiful center of peace within you that was never actually lost but is simply yet unclaimed?

e5: You tend to think you can fill your inner emptiness solely with ideas. You fear that too much life "out there" will never fulfill but only drain you—too much intensity of others' needs or emotions, too much exertion of your energy in doing. What would happen, however, if you emptied yourself of endless knowledge-seeking and left your inner castle unguarded? What would occur if you let the current of life, including other people's energies, wash through your inner chambers and sometimes carry you away? Would you feel empty then?

e6: Your conditioned belief is that trusting leads to catastrophe, so you send fear ahead of you as a vigilant scout and guardian. The problem is that our attention will always find what it is looking for. What would happen, however, if you sent out different surveyors that could see and hold a larger truth? What if, through the eyes of faith, you could hold an unwavering gaze at the world's sufferings but also its joys, failures, and triumphs? What would happen if you dared to trust human evolution, including your own life's unfolding?

e7: Your insistence on being carefree is too often inspired by an inner sadness, rather than a bursting joy. Even the term *carefree* suggests its source: your experience of being without nurturing care. What would happen if you stopped being antisocial and went with the pack? What if you dared to stop worrying about securing your own pleasure and avoiding pain? What if you felt the blessing of letting that mind rest in your heart or in the care of another?

e8: Your fear of being wounded keeps your heart more vulnerable than most. The sweetest, most tender part of you never has the chance to know its strength because it stays so well armored against rejection and betrayal. What if your Worldly Warrior met your Inner Child? What if they agreed to work together and learn from one another for your highest good? What if the world could see both aspects of you at the same time? What if you could see other people and things in the same way, and less as either good or evil or black and white?

e9: Embracing conflict is one of the most tremendous gifts you can give to yourself. What looks like sloth may be the result of sheer fatigue from resisting 24/7, any personal views that might disturb the peace. Attention to your own feelings and opinions may feel horrifying at first because it will likely bring up your feelings of anger and personal insignificance. What would happen, however, if you accepted your negative feelings and let yourself feel them in your body with compassion rather than judgment? What would happen if you spoke your truth?

Reflect: What insights did you gain from your type's activation? Did you experience any fears or resistance? Elaborate.

> *We are daily bombarded with new information as to the nature of reality. If we are to incorporate this information, we must continually revise our maps, and sometimes when enough new information has accumulated, we must make very major revisions. The process of making revisions, particularly major revisions, is painful, sometimes excruciatingly painful. And herein lies the major source of many of the ills of mankind.*
>
> —M. Scott Peck, *The Road Less Traveled*

What Matters Most

Cat: Where are you going?
Alice: Which way should I go?
Cat: That depends on where you are going.
Alice: I don't know.
Cat: Then it doesn't matter which way you go.

—Lewis Carroll, *Alice's Adventures in Wonderland*

And every day, the world will drag you by the hand, yelling, "This is important! And this is important! And this is important! You need to worry about this! And this! And this!" And each day, it's up to you to yank your hand back, put it on your heart and say, "No. This is what's important."

—Iain Thomas, author of *I Wrote This for You*

Many of us can stay perpetually busy yet lack a sense of deeper purpose, meaning, or fulfillment. This is in part because when we neglect to carve the time and space to remember what matters most, we can easily get lost in the habits of our Ennea-type—which might include compulsive working, irresistible helping, or incessant ruminating. We might often find that we are steadily occupied yet not quite sure where our time goes each day. Some of us spend the bulk of our days in chronic overwhelm or ennui.

It is important to pause and ask: *Where am I even headed? Am I going in circles? Do I even care about the destination I seem to be headed toward if I continue this course of action (or protracted inaction)?*

This activation is about making space to discern your soul's true path and next steps. Let yourself open to a life that is about more than just making it from one day to the next, one deadening routine to the next, or one unfulfilling task to the next. You can enjoy a lifegiving, soulful existence if you are willing to make space to discern the nudging of your inmost self. Remember: All you need is already within you.

Activation by Type

e1: You can become so fixated on perfecting or correcting what is right in front of you that you lose sight of the bigger, long-term picture. Make space today to imagine your highest visions coming into fruition. Discern what attitudes and behaviors are—and aren't—serving this greater purpose. Then be willing to bear the discomfort of leaving certain issues unresolved, so you can stay on mission in a larger way.

e2: You can experience such overwhelm from taking on others' problems as your own that you readily excuse yourself from the responsibility of discerning and then living your own life's purpose (allowing yourself to consider it might be something beyond your care for others). Make space to attend to your dreams, personal ambitions, and creative pursuits. Recognize you need not wait for loved ones to get their acts together or show up as you'd hope before you can move forward with your own life. Be willing to let others down to stand up for yourself.

e3: You can become so identified with how things seem that you forget to drop beneath appearances to ask yourself how you actually are. Make space today to inquire patiently and compassionately into your true feelings and wants—even if that means allowing for feelings of overwhelm, anxiety, shame, or depression. Letting yourself show up less put together for a season can help you to make better choices for a richer, more personally rewarding life.

e4: You can wander so far into the forest of the past it becomes difficult to feel your way in the dark back to the present. How can you make empowered decisions when you feel so lost? The process of bringing compassionate awareness to the sensations you are experiencing in your physical body in this moment is like holding up a lantern. Suddenly, you are brought immediately and directly back home to yourself. In this moment, you know what is true for you and you have the power to act from that truth.

e5: You have a protective habit of over-restricting needs and desires, which can lead to deprivation rather than the sustenance and nourishment you seek. Likely, you have felt rejected in the past, and your needs or desires were unmet, so you decided to guard your heart by minimizing your real needs, whether physical or emotional. Be willing to investigate whether there are dreams or wishes you locked into a room inside yourself. Consider unlocking that door because a gift there will most likely help you know something about where you have been, where you are now, and which direction to take next in life.

e6: You can become so hypervigilant guarding against future dangers that it becomes nearly impossible for you to plan for any future joy. Wise decision-making demands you take a leap of faith—to trust the good in the universe as well as in your own inner knowing. For this to happen, however, you must first grant your mind permission to take leave of its guard post. Then send it out to scout courageously for positive possibilities.

e7: You can become so preoccupied with mentally imagining the next new experience that you fail to see the good that is right in front of you. Slowing down your thoughts and actions can feel stifling, but only because doing so brings up fear, which is hidden right beneath the surface of your attention. Only when you are willing to feel your fear along with other difficult feelings from your past, such as grief or anger, can you make wonderfully wise, life-giving decisions that are not unconsciously driven by old wounds you've never given yourself room to heal.

e8: You can wreak substantial havoc when you willfully refuse to slow down and temper your shoot-first, ask-later mentality. Your need for intensity keeps you actively plowing forward without much reflection on whether an equally effective way might be less damaging to your surroundings or your health. Discernment requires not only patience but also the willingness to consider your past actions, including your mistakes, and to feel in your heart the pain that is likely buried there from past hurts, rejections, or betrayals.

e9: You can become so attached to inner calm that you refuse to allow any new experiences to disturb this semblance of peace. This means rather than take any bold action toward self-assertion or self-expression, you often prefer to live in a kind of reverie, reminiscing about the past and occasionally fantasizing about what might happen in the future. Discerning what constitutes right action for you requires that you are willing to accept impacting and being impacted by others.

Reflect: Were you able to pause from your preoccupations to gain clarity on your deepest passions and purpose? If you struggled to clear space for discernment, can you sense why that might be? Sometimes, we are afraid to gain clarity because we fear what it might mean for our current life and relationships. Sometimes, we fear there is nothing important within us. What obstacles arose as you considered your passions and purpose?

Note that discernment is an ongoing practice that requires time and patience. If you are not accustomed to listening for your own truth, or if you simply have not checked in with yourself in a long while, consider staying with this practice for a few weeks.

Things which matter most must never be
at the mercy of things which matter least.

— Johann Wolfgang von Goethe, German polymath and writer

Let It Be

We are constantly trying to hold it all together.
If you really want to see why you do things,
then don't do them and see what happens.

—Michael A. Singer, *The Untethered Soul*

If we want to know whether we are truly exercising free will each day rather than letting the habits of our ego dictate our choices and schedule, all we need to do is experiment with letting something be undone, unsaid, or unmade that we have customarily insisted must happen. Often the challenge of attempting this intentional self-restraint is humbling. Certainly, it is illuminating. What will you simply let be today?

Activation by Type

e1: What disordered situation or disturbing flaw can you leave uncorrected today? Notice with compassionate curiosity what comes up inside you when you do this. How strong is your compulsion to improve or fix? How often do you succumb to it? How often do you resist it? How often does acting on it leave you feeling righteous or resentful?

e2: What advice or assistance can you resist offering today? Notice with compassionate curiosity what comes up inside you when you do this. How immediate is your tendency to offer your services or counsel? How often do you succumb to it? How often do you resist it? How often does acting on it leave you feeling prideful or unappreciated?

e3: What item on your task list can you leave undone today? Notice with compassionate curiosity what comes up inside you when you do this. How strong is your urge to be productive 24/7 with times of rest simply being a means to accomplishing more? How often does your busyness leave you feeling empty or out of touch with your own heart?

e4: What would happen if you let yourself be one in a crowd today, not needing to be seen as special or unique? Notice with compassionate curiosity what comes up inside you when you do this. How intense is your need to do or share something to make sure you stand out? How often do you succumb to it? How often do you resist it? How often does acting on it leave you feeling more separate or shameful?

e5: What rabbit hole of research can you resist going down today so you can spend time engaging relationally with others? Notice with compassionate curiosity what comes up inside you when you do this. How pressing is your tendency to withdraw into the world of collecting and synthesizing ideas? How often do you succumb to it? How often do you resist it? How often does acting on it leave you feeling emptier, lonelier, and/or more disillusioned?

e6: What decisions can you make today without needing to canvass others' opinions? Notice with compassionate curiosity what comes up inside you when you do this. How acute is your tendency to second-guess your own judgment? How often do you succumb to seeking external support? How often do you resist that tendency? To what extent does over-reliance on others cause you to feel even more generally anxious and more doubting of your own intuition?

e7: What would happen if you sank into a painful memory or experience today? Notice with compassionate curiosity what comes up inside you when you do this. How quick is your impulse to run from pain in the pursuit of pleasure? How often do you surrender to that impulse? How often do you resist it? Does your appetite for pleasure ever feel sated or do you constantly crave something new or something more?

e8: What would happen if you let someone off the hook for an injustice today? Notice with compassionate curiosity what comes up inside you when you do this. How immediate is your urge to take control, mete out punishment, or otherwise right the wrong? How often do you succumb to this tendency? How often do you resist it? How often does acting on it leave you feeling more hardened, less joyful, and less trusting of the world?

e9: Can you let differences simply be present without trying to bring harmony or unanimity to the situation? Instead of peace-making, what difficult conversation can you face and engage in today? Notice with compassionate curiosity what comes up inside you when you do this. How immediate is your tendency to back off or capitulate just to keep the peace? How often in your life do you succumb to this tendency?

How often do you resist it? How often does acting on it leave you feeling unimportant or invisible?

Reflect: How effective were you at resisting the types of actions specified for your type? What fears or concerns came up for you in this exercise? If you overcame those fears or concerns, what helped you do so?

Breathe and let be.

—Jon Kabat-Zinn, *Wherever You Go, There You Are*

DAY 38

Refreshment and Renewal

*Fueled by faith and passion for our true priorities we're
going to drive against traffic in order to find rest,
refreshment, and time for what matters most in life.*

—Craig Groeschel, *Weird*

*Do not be conformed to this world, but be
transformed by the renewing of your mind.*

—Romans 12:2

This activation is about intentionally making space for refreshment along our journey.
Although in some cases this might mean physical rest, in others inspired activity in
line with your dreams and passions might be what your soul has been sorely missing.
Likewise, although it is sometimes the case that renewal requires doing things differently, it might simply mean taking on a new perspective. Remember that spiritual
renewal involves the grace-filled work of Spirit more than the hard efforts of your ego.

Activation by Type

e1: *What activity would lighten my heart (even if it feels frivolous or indulgent to
do it)?*

e2: *What steps might I take toward a personal goal or desire (even if it feels selfish to
focus on me)?*

e3: *What choice might I make to honor what I'm feeling or needing at this time (even
if it feels nonproductive)?*

e4: *What three things can I appreciate out loud about myself (even if doing this might
bring up shame)?*

e5: *Where might I practice generosity (even if it brings up my fears of depletion and
scarcity)?*

e6: *Where might I be more playful (even if it might feel irresponsible to relax into the
joy of any given moment)?*

e7: *What might I give my all to (even if it means missing out on other options)?*

e8: *Where might I allow myself to experience tenderness and gentleness (even if it means feeling vulnerable)?*

e9: *Where might I make time for a fun and engaging activity (in which I am an active participant and not just a spectator)?*

Reflect: Were you able to accept this invitation to rest and refresh? Elaborate on what the experience was like for you and what gifts this activation might hold for your ongoing journey. Can you sense how rest is not just a ground for sustained action—it also fosters a space for mystical connection?

> *Rest invites us to touch our own innate value and dignity*
> *as creatures on this planet. More than replenishment,*
> *rest opens into creativity, joy, and the mystical.*
>
> —Oren Jay Sofer, *Your Heart Was Made for This*

DAY 39

Reframing Your Values

What is success? . . . It is being able to go
to bed each night with your soul at peace.

—Paulo Coelho, *Manuscript Found in Accra*

As we evolve, there comes a time when it makes sense to redefine or reframe our goals and values—what I like to think of as our life quests. For example, what success means to me as a Type 3 has *drastically* changed. When I was in my teens, it meant financial success, fame, and adulation. Now it means inner peace, a sense of passion and purpose, and fulfilling relationships.

At this point in your journey, chances are you have a new perspective on life—on what matters most. What do the terms most often related to your Ennea-type (concepts such as perfection, service, power, harmony, etc.) mean to you? How have their meanings changed?

Activation by Type

e1: Living in integrity is not about striving toward some ideal outside yourself. Rather, it is about fully embracing your authentic nature and trusting that, as you accept every part of your humanity, you express a divine radiance more profoundly loving than any outer teaching or code of conduct could ever engender.

e2: Being a light for others is not about being another's hero or savior. Rather, it is about shining your own light so brightly that others see themselves more clearly in your presence. Rather than expend all your energy trying to help others up their mountains of challenge, focus on climbing your own. The higher you rise, the more naturally and effortlessly you serve as a beacon of hope for those around you.

e3: Claiming your personal value is not an end goal to be achieved at some finish line that seems to be pushed back each day. Rather, it involves a moment-to-moment clarity of heart that enables you to consistently value—and to affirmatively choose—your personal feelings and needs over any outer recognition. In truth, you have already arrived; you are already worthy.

e4: Being special is not about standing apart, even though it can feel that way. Rather, when you recognize that every single person is unique—yourself included—you see how this is simply a fact of life. Each person has a precious originality that does not need to conform to the world to fully belong to it. No matter what you might fantasize, you cannot escape your intrinsic and exquisite belonging.

e5: Your quest for competency cannot merely be a thought experiment. Only when you relinquish the rabbit holes of relentless knowledge-seeking in favor of concrete action, interactive relationships, and embodied experiences will you realize you were born with everything you need for a rich and full life.

e6: Cultivating an experience of safety and security is not primarily an outside job. Rather, it is an experience best resourced from the inside. As you anchor yourself to your own inner knowing, you can access an enlarged sense of strength, stability, and surety, which serves to bolster your loftiest dreams and everyday decision-making.

e7: The pursuit of happiness is incomplete when it neglects to embrace life's ups and downs. Your true bliss involves freely surfing the waves of challenge and joy, knowing the less you struggle, the more buoyant you are. Even more deeply, when you're faithful enough to still your mind and settle your heart, you realize you cannot really drown beneath even the greatest tsunami of sadness. This is because the whole ocean, from its depths to its surface, is all actually you.

e8: Being powerful is not about being fiercely independent. Rather, true strength involves knowing when to be brave enough to dare to let someone in, to risk having someone impact your heart, to test your belief that you cannot lean on anyone but yourself. Because you are tough and resilient, you can choose to be open to others in the present moment, even if you've been betrayed in the past.

e9: Harmony does not require consensus or conformity. True peace, unity, and oneness come from your willingness to embrace your different and even conflicting desires and opinions without withdrawing from yourself or the world. Because caring for everyone means caring for yourself, give yourself permission to take up space in your own awareness and, unapologetically, in the lives of those around you.

Reflect: What insights did you gain from this practice of "reframing" the core values of your type? Are there other terms you've related to throughout your life that also need to be updated? In what ways have some of your most basic assumptions and perspectives on life changed since embarking on this contemplative Enneagram journey?

> *There are things known and there are things unknown,*
> *and in between are the doors of perception.*

> —Aldous Huxley, *The Doors of Perception*

At the End of the Day

*At the end of the day, right now, right here, wherever you are,
you can make a choice to be present and happy and fulfilled.*

—Eric Lange, American actor

This activation is about letting yourself feel a sense of arrival and homecoming. There is *always* more that you might do, learn, feel, or accomplish, but give yourself some props here. There is no such thing as doing life perfectly. You will never achieve all there might be to achieve in life.

Your efforts are pointless if you keep postponing peace or presence until a future condition is met or an imagined time has come. In this moment, feel your seat in the chair and your feet on the floor. Notice how your breath nourishes your body. Sense the beating of your heart. Give yourself permission to come to peace with who and where you are in this sacred moment of your aliveness. Be here now.

Activation by Type:

e1: At the end of the day, remember to make peace with yourself, trusting that even if your efforts seemed imperfect by your high standards, your best truly was good enough.

e2: At the end of the day, remember that creating time and space to tend to your own needs is not selfish. You are as worthy of affection and care as anyone else.

e3: At the end of the day, remember to check in with your heart. Treat yourself as beloved, no matter what you accomplished or didn't accomplish on this day.

e4: At the end of the day, remember to practice gratitude for all that you have, recognizing that your life has its unique challenges and joys—a path authentic to you and incomparable to that of any others.

e5: At the end of the day, remember to relax your quest to fully understand or know a particular topic. Honor the expertise that you already possess and grant space for the inevitable unknowns that are woven into our human existence.

e6: At the end of the day, remember to bear witness to your own courage and goodness. Often, the valiant efforts you make for others are invisible to them. Let that be okay.

e7: At the end of the day, remember to review the past twenty-four hours rather than jumping impatiently to future-planning. Dwell especially on the moments when you experienced joy, beauty, contentment, or satisfaction. Let those memories fill your heart.

e8: At the end of the day, remember to give yourself permission to ask for support. As strong as you are, you are made stronger by the care you are willing to let in.

e9: At the end of the day, remember that it's okay to have differences in perspective with those around you. Stand up for your own opinions while embracing a sense of unity that includes the full spectrum of our amazing diversity.

Reflect: What if there is really nothing more you need to be or do right here and right now?

Breathing in, I calm body and mind.
Breathing out, I smile.
Dwelling in the present moment, I know this is the only moment.

—Thích Nhất Hạnh, *Being Peace*

APPENDIX A

Evolving Together: A Guide for Groups

It has been my joy to discover that the intersection of conscious community, the Enneagram, and contemplative practice creates a sacred space to inspire and nourish our spiritual lives in a world thirsting for authentic and loving connection. If you are inspired to work through this book with another person or a group of people, here are a few guidelines to consider.[1]

Preparation

STEP 1: Gather your fellow Enneagram soul-journers—online or in person!

I recommend that you support no more than fifteen to twenty people per group. If there are just two or three of you, you might want to alternate who facilitates the meeting so you have a sense of mutuality.

STEP 2: Decide on the frequency and duration of your shared commitment to this journey.

Base this on whether you wish to journey through this entire book together or select certain portions. If you meet weekly, you can have individuals explore one activation per day or one per week. Ideally, meet weekly or, at minimum, every two weeks. Groups can lose momentum and accountability with longer breaks between meetings. If your meetings involve eating or socializing, keep that part separate from the reflection and spiritual practice time, as grounded attentiveness is a vital component to the group's individual and collective transformation.

STEP 3: One day or one week before you meet, invite everyone to read and reflect on the section(s) of the book you will be exploring in advance of the meeting.

For those newer to Enneagram inner work, you might consider starting at the beginning. Others might jump directly to the activations.

Group Guidelines

These guidelines are vital to fostering sacred space. Note, however, that they are *not* meant to be enforced harshly. If someone breaks a guideline once, you might mention something outside the group meeting to avoid shaming them. Sometimes I wait a few shares and then make a friendly and gentle reminder about the guidelines and their value to cultivating safe, sacred space.

NO CROSS TALK.[2] *Cross talk* means we address others "across" the room. Examples of cross talk include speaking directly to another person rather than to the facilitator or generally to the group, advising others, questioning or interrupting the person who is speaking, and making judgments (whether positive or negative) about what someone else shared. Although ideally each of us is impacted by what is shared in a group, the key is to focus not on the speaker, but on your own experience. For instance, responding to a share with: "You are so courageous!" is cross talk. Instead, reflect on how the share impacted you personally. For instance, you might say: "When so-and-so shared about her pilgrimage walking El Camino, I felt inspired because I've been fearful about taking an important step in my life. I feel more courage to brave the challenges that might come up for me now." By avoiding cross talk, we accept what others say as true for them. We also practice being present not only to the other person but also to what is arising in ourselves—a vital element for our inner work.

NO INTERRUPTIONS. This guideline is technically included in the No Cross Talk guideline, but it is important enough to warrant special mention. When meeting online, remind people that using the Chat feature during someone's share constitutes an interruption since we are essentially speaking rather than listening during the share. You may want to discourage the use of Chat during the meeting entirely as it detracts from attentive listening and can lead to side conversations.

STRICT CONFIDENTIALITY. Even if members of a group are close friends or partners, whatever a person shares in circle must stay in circle. Consider it a prayer circle where some may choose to share a very intimate part of themselves as a way of surrendering it to Spirit's wisdom and care. Unless someone explicitly says you can bring up their share outside a group, don't do it! Only the person who shared has the right to bring it up again.

SILENCE IS WELCOME. Make sure the group knows that periods of silence are welcome. No one needs to jump in to fill the silence. Times of silence in community are sometimes rare but can be some of the richest moments together. In fact, when the silence becomes awkward, this is an excellent opportunity for you to notice your own discomfort and see what happens when you stay with yourself. Also, different types share in different ways. Those who tend to be quieter will not share if the more assertive types always jump in and fill up the silence.

COME AS YOU ARE. Invite participants not to leave their feelings or what is most pressing for them at the door when they enter the circle. Healing comes when we bring what is truly alive for us and allow it to be witnessed compassionately by others.

Facilitating the Circle

STEP 1: Begin by facilitating a centering and grounding practice that supports presence.

Check out "Nine Practices" for ideas. Grounding (Practice 4) and Inner Observer (Practice 3) are great choices for opening the circle. If you're a skilled meditation leader, you may want to introduce your own short, guided meditation to support the theme of the day.

STEP 2: Introduce the day's theme and open the circle for a time of open sharing (without pressuring anyone to share).

You might begin with a passage from your selected reading or use one of the reflection questions offered at the end of each activation. You can also lead with open-ended questions such as: "What's alive for you (around this theme or in your life in general)?" or "What comes up for you around your type's activation?"

STEP 3: After folks have had a chance to check in (usually around thirty minutes into the meeting), engage in a twenty-minute Centering Prayer (Practice 1) sit.[3]

It is the practice as much as the sharing that supports spiritual transformation.

A Word of Caution

Inner work will inevitably bring up any unresolved trauma or other wounding. Often, this means that individuals need resources beyond what a contemplative Enneagram group or group leader can provide. An ethical group facilitator (or one-on-one mentor) will stay in their own lane and will make a referral when they observe that a person is struggling with basic self-regulation in group or that their needs are otherwise outside the scope of the facilitator's expertise. For instance, as a pastoral counselor and spiritual mentor who is not a therapist, I will make a referral when I see that trauma, addiction, or other type of therapy work may be needed before the person can benefit from, or safely proceed in, the inner work described in this book (in a group or otherwise). Although layperson facilitators are not bound by professional ethical duties, it is important that participants and facilitators are all aware of these considerations so they can continue to maximize individual and group safety and effectiveness.

On a related note, when looking for an Enneagram guide (for one-on-one or group work), know that the Enneagram community is not regulated (like, say, the practice of medicine is in the United States). Technically, anyone can call themselves an Enneagram coach or expert. It is important to consider how long that person has been studying the Enneagram, what other relevant background they have, and whether that would-be expert is certified with an established Enneagram program or school, or whether they have earned the status of being an International Enneagram Association (IEA) Accredited Professional.[4]

Tips for the Nine Types of Participants

The compulsion of type is strong. As we embark on this journey, our ego's type structure will instinctually try to direct our behavior toward a safe and familiar harbor. Here are a few tips to support each type in surrendering control of its growth process, thereby allowing room for grace.

e1: Practice showing up even when you feel raw, messy, or imperfect and risk sharing even when your thoughts feel unformed and disorganized. Remember to check your default thinking that inner work is for "fixing" what you believe is wrong or broken (particularly with yourself). Rather, consider that the spiritual journey is about embodying the truth that you are already inherently whole and perfect.

e2: Practice using "I" statements when you share. Talk about what is going on for you, including *your* needs and feelings—especially the ones that embarrass you. While focusing on yourself can feel uncomfortable and selfish, doing so is what you need to do to uncover your authentic self. Find relief in the group guidelines, which forbid unsolicited advice-giving, thereby allowing you to relax and trust that it's not your job to help or fix others in the group. By leaning into this, you will learn how to feel loved even when you aren't actively needed!

e3: Practice sharing without shape-shifting or carefully curating everything you will say. This will help to offset your type's tendency to seek admiration as a proxy for authentic love and connection. Also, do your best to relinquish the attitude that you are in the group to grow or make progress. Instead, you're practicing being rather than always doing. Embrace the fundamental truth: you are worthy exactly as you are today!

e4: Notice when you start to make judgments, rating yourself as either less than or better than others in the group. See if you can listen without needing to put anyone else above or below you. Also, practice listening to others with curiosity for their unique experience, without always relating it back to yourself. This way, you begin to cultivate greater understanding and compassion, which will give you a deepened sense of authentic connection and belonging. Check your tendency to look for evidence that you don't belong, that no one understands you, or that your suffering is unique. You are *naturally* beautiful and special. Practice being curious about your commonalities rather than your differences.

e5: Your default tendency is to sit back and observe rather than fully participate and engage. When you do engage, you are most comfortable sharing facts or ideas. Try getting out of your comfort zone by sharing personal stories and feelings with the group. The ability to share more personally gets easier with practice! Realize that putting down the drawbridge and stepping out from behind your castle walls can bring you life-giving, heartfelt nourishment.

e6: Practice trusting yourself and releasing the need for everyone else to understand you or assure you that you are okay. Remember to check your tendency to project your negative thoughts and feelings onto others. Notice your anxiety and bring silent compassion to yourself as you bravely share your own truth. See if you can share your joys as well as your fears and concerns. Realize in your heart that others may care for you more than your mind is likely to tell you they do.

e7: Even though routines can often feel confining for you, try to be as consistent in your group attendance as possible. After all, when you don't show up in a committed way, you miss out on a lot of the blessings the group dynamic offers over time. And they also miss out on you! Listen from your heart rather than merely thinking about or analyzing what is being shared by others. When you catch yourself getting impatient or drifting into your plans or imagination, gently bring your attention back to the present moment by sensing your feet on the ground. Remember that life is never in the future or somewhere else. It only ever happens in the here and now!

e8: Practice listening more than sharing—listening not only to others but to what is happening within your own heart. Temper your tendency to jump in to manage or control the process as a way of staying armored and invulnerable. Imagine taking off your armor as you begin each meeting. Remind yourself that softness is a strength and sharing your vulnerability with others is one of the most powerful and transformational things you can do.

e9: Practice keeping to "I" rather than lapsing into "we" statements. Remember that you have a unique life perspective and experience that is worthy of sharing. Let yourself take up space and time in the group! Notice your habit of checking out and missing important details of others' shares. Practice staying attentive and actively engaged, both when you are speaking and when you're listening. Check your compulsion around trying to maintain ease and harmony at any cost. Remember that some discomfort and disharmony are essential to your finding a sense of authentic peace and selfhood.

Contemplative Enneagram Resources

Enneagram Tests

Here are reputable online Enneagram tests for your self-typing discovery journey. Remember that an online test is not definitive of type but can be a helpful piece of information. I strongly advise that you read Enneagram books and work with an Enneagram mentor in addition to taking any of these type indicators.

- RHETI: https://www.enneagraminstitute.com/
- WEPSS: https://www.wepss.com/
- IEQ9: https://www.integrative9.com/

Recommendations for Those New to the Enneagram

Enneagram Fundamentals

Daniels, David, and Virginia Price. *The Essential Enneagram: The Definitive Personality Test and Self-Discovery Guide—Revised and Updated.* New York: HarperOne, 2009.

Maitri, Sandra. *The Spiritual Dimension of the Enneagram: Nine Faces of the Soul.* New York: Penguin Putnam, 2000.

Riso, Don Richard, and Russ Hudson. *The Wisdom of the Enneagram: The Complete Guide to Psychological and Spiritual Growth for the Nine Personality Types.* New York: Bantam, 1999.

For Learning Differing Perspectives About the Instinctual Drives

Chestnut, Beatrice. *The Complete Enneagram: 27 Paths to Greater Self-Knowledge.* Berkeley, CA: She Writes Press, 2013.

Luckovich, John. *The Instinctual Drives and the Enneagram.* Self-published, 2021.

Bibliography and Recommended Reading

Almaas, A.H. *Facets of Unity: The Enneagram of Holy Ideas.* Boston: Shambhala Publications, 1998.

—————. *Keys to the Enneagram: How to Unlock the Highest Potential of Every Personality Type*. Boston: Shambhala Publications, 2021.

Bast, Mary, and Clarence Thomson. *Out of the Box: Coaching with the Enneagram*. New Mexico: Ninestar Publishing, 2005.

Beattie, Melody. *The Language of Letting Go: Daily Meditations for Codependents*. Danvers, MA: Hazelden Publishing, 1990.

Bourgeault, Cynthia. *Centering Prayer and Inner Awakening*. Lanham, MD: Cowley Publications, 2004. Kindle.

—————. *The Heart of Centering Prayer: Nondual Christianity in Theory and Practice*. Boulder, CO: Shambhala Publications, 2016.

—————. *The Holy Trinity and the Law of Three: Discovering the Radical Truth at the Heart of Christianity*. Boston: Shambhala Publications, 2013.

Bowen, Sarah, and Alan Marlatt. "Surfing the Urge: Brief Mindfulness-based Intervention for College Student Smokers." *Psychology of Addictive Behaviors* 23, no. 4 (December 2009): 666–71. https://doi.org/10.1037/a0017127.

Brown, Brené. *Atlas of the Heart: Mapping Meaningful Connection and the Language of Human Experience*. New York: Random House, 2021.

Brumet, Robert. *Birthing a Greater Reality: A Guide for Conscious Evolution*. Lee's Summit, MO: Unity, 2010.

Chestnut, Beatrice. *The Complete Enneagram: 27 Paths to Greater Self-Knowledge*. Berkeley, CA: She Writes Press, 2013.

—————. *The Enneagram System's 27 Personality Subtypes*. Self-published, 2012.

Contemplative Outreach. "Centering Prayer." n.d. https://www.contemplativeout reach.org.

Covey, Stephen. *The 7 Habits of Highly Effective People*. New York: Simon and Schuster, 1999.

Daniels, David N., and Virginia A. Price. *The Essential Enneagram: The Definitive Personality Test and Self-Discovery Guide—Revised and Updated*. New York: HarperOne, 2009.

Empereur, James. *The Enneagram and Spiritual Direction: Nine Paths to Spiritual Guidance*. New York: Bloomsbury Academic, 1990.

Fox, Matthew. *Original Blessing: A Primer in Creation Spirituality*. New York: Tarcher Perigee, 2000.

Furey, Robert J. *The Joy of Kindness*. Chestnut Ridge, NY: Crossroad, 1993.

Goldberg, Natalie. *The True Secret of Writing: Connecting Life with Language (A Gift for Writers)*. New York: Atria Books, 2013.

————. *Writing Down the Bones: Freeing the Writer Within*. Boulder, CO: Shambhala Publications, 2006.

Hendrix, Harville. *Getting the Love You Want: A Guide for Couples*. New York: Henry Holt and Co., 2007.

Heuertz, Christopher L. *The Enneagram of Belonging: A Compassionate Journey of Self-Acceptance*. Michigan: Zondervan, 2020.

————. *The Sacred Enneagram: Finding Your Unique Path to Spiritual Growth*. Michigan: Zondervan, 2017.

Hudson, Russ. *The Enneagram: Nine Gateways to Presence*. Louisville, CO: Sounds True, 2021. Audio book.

Hurley, Kathleen, and Theodore Dobson. *My Best Self: Using the Enneagram to Free the Soul*. New York: HarperOne, 1993.

Keating, Thomas. *Open Mind, Open Heart*. London: Bloomsbury Continuum, 2006.

Keltner, Dacher. *Awe: The New Science of Everyday Wonder and How It Can Transform Your Life*. New York: Penguin Publishing Group, 2024. Kindle edition.

Maitri, Sandra. *The Enneagram of Passions and Virtues: Finding the Way Home*. New York: Penguin, 2005.

————. *The Spiritual Dimension of the Enneagram: Nine Faces of the Soul*. New York: Penguin Putnam, 2000.

Metz, Barbara, and John Burchill. *The Enneagram and Prayer: Discovering Our True Selves Before God*. Denville, NJ: Dimension Books, 1987.

Mohan, A. G., with Ganesh Mohan. "Memories of a Master." *Yoga Journal*, September 2, 2021. https://www.yogajournal.com.

Moser, Drew. *The Enneagram of Discernment: The Way of Vocation, Wisdom, and Practice*. Beaver Falls, PA: Falls City Press, 2020.

Naranjo, Claudio. *Ennea-Type Structures: Self-Analysis for the Seeker*. Nevada City, CA: Gateways Books and Tapes, 1990.

Palmer, Helen. *The Enneagram in Love and Work: Understanding Your Intimate and Business Relationships*. New York: HarperOne, 1995.

Pilar. "What Is the Meaning of Anjali Mudra?" Bodhi Surf Yoga. May 27, 2020. https://www.bodhisurfyoga.com.

Rea, Shiva. "What Is Anjali Mudra?" *Yoga Journal*, June 6, 2024. https://www.yoga journal.com.

Riley, Cole Arthur. *This Here Flesh: Spirituality, Liberation, and the Stories That Make Us.* New York: Random House, 2023.

Riso, Don Richard, and Russ Hudson. *The Wisdom of the Enneagram: The Complete Guide to Psychological and Spiritual Growth for the Nine Personality Types.* New York: Bantam, 1999.

Robins, Abi. *The Conscious Enneagram: How to Move from Typology to Transformation.* Minneapolis, MN: Broadleaf Books, 2021.

Rohr, Richard. "Gratitude and Generosity." *The Daily Meditations.* Center for Action and Contemplation. November 22, 2022. https://cac.org.

Rohr, Richard, and Andreas Ebert. *The Enneagram: A Christian Perspective.* Translated by Peter Heinegg. New York: Crossroad, 2006.

Schafer, William. *Roaming Free Inside the Cage: A Daoist Approach to the Enneagram and Spiritual Transformation.* Self-published: Iuniverse, 2010.

Timms, Moira. *Beyond Prophecies and Predictions: Everyone's Guide to the Coming Changes.* New York: Ballantine Books, 1996.

Unity. "About Affirmative Prayer." n.d. https://www.unity.org.

———. Unity Five-Step Prayer Process." n.d. https://www.unity.org.

Zuercher, Suzanne. *Enneagram Spirituality: From Compulsion to Contemplation.* Notre Dame, IN: Ave Maria Press, 1992.

———. *Using the Enneagram in Prayer: A Contemplative Guide.* Notre Dame, IN: Ave Maria Press, 2008.

NOTES

Introduction

1. For more about Unity, visit www.unity.org.
2. IEANinePoints, "IEA ADPs."
3. The RHETI, which stands for Riso-Hudson Enneagram Type Indicator, is a scientifically-validated test instrument developed by Don Riso and Russ Hudson and is now considered a standard test in the Enneagram field. See Appendix B for a link to this and other reputable Enneagram indicators.
4. Maitri, *Spiritual Dimension of Enneagram*, 23–41.
5. Maitri, *Spiritual Dimension of Enneagram*, 26.
6. Almaas, *Facets of Unity*.
7. It is important to note here that the names commonly used to refer to each Enneagram type can vary substantially in the Enneagram literature. This is partly because the original Enneagram is based on a numbering system. The names were later assigned by various teachers to offer a shortcut to the type that described one of the type's core characteristics. The hazard of this is that folks new to the Enneagram latch onto that one word or phrase used to name a type and then think they are that type because they identify with the word or phrase. Be careful not to confuse the name for the type. For instance, someone might think, "I'm a Perfectionist! Therefore, I must be a Type 1." (In fact, I made that mistake myself at the outset of my Enneagram journey!) It turns out that many Enneagram types can have highly perfectionistic traits. More core to whether you are a particular Ennea-type is not what you do (perfectionistic behavior) but why you do it (to perfect/correct life [Type 1], to be regarded as outstanding [Type 3], to keep the peace [Type 9], and so forth). (See "Principle 3: Type Is Rooted in Motivation, Not Behavior.")

Part I: Nine Principles, Nine Practices, Nine Prayers

Nine Principles

1. The original source of this truism is unknown. This proposition has recently been attributed to French theologian Pierre Teilhard de Chardin in Furey, *The Joy of Kindness*, 138, as well as to Gurdjieff in Timms, *Beyond Prophecies and Predictions*, 62.
2. If you are interested in a Christian perspective that holds that we were born in original blessing rather than in original sin, I recommend Fox's *Original Blessing*.
3. Rohr and Ebert, *The Enneagram*.

4. "e" followed by the numeral stands for "Enneagram type [number]." These abbreviations will be used in each of the forty activations in Part II.

5. Even back in the heyday of the self-help movement, Stephen Covey, author of the *New York Times* bestselling book, *7 Habits of Highly Effective People*, wrote that modern culture overvalues independence and devalues interdependence. He sequenced the seven habits to guide practitioners along the "Maturity Continuum" from dependence to independence to interdependence—interdependence being a more "mature" state because it aligns more with reality. For Covey, interdependent people can take care of their own needs, but they also recognize that a collaborative relationship is greater than the sum of its parts. See Covey, *7 Habits of Highly Effective People*.

6. The complexity of subtypes is beyond the scope of this Enneagram guide but significant enough to warrant mention here. A subtype is your core Enneagram type flavored by your dominant instinctual bias. I have seen and experienced that although knowing your dominant instinctual bias and how you prioritize the three instinctual domains is exceedingly helpful in the inner journey, the activations in this book are designed to get at the core of each of the nine primary Enneagram types so that you do not need to know your subtype. To support your education and enrichment on this important topic, however, see Appendix B for recommended readings.

7. Oneness is, of course, not limited to the oneness of humans, but of all life. That said, the focus of this principle is on the way inner work is supported by practicing inner work within the context of our greater human family, not on further elevating humans above the rest of life but on grappling with other humans in a way that, ultimately, we come to see our own wholeness and belonging more clearly. For leading-edge work in "rewilding" the Enneagram, check out Ben Campbell's work at www.wildenneagram.com.

8. Robins, *Conscious Enneagram*.

9. If you are interested in getting involved in an Evolving Enneagram group, find us at www.evolvingenneagram.com. If you are interested in leading your own community, see Appendix A for guidance on facilitating—*and participating in*—small groups using *The Enneagram of the Soul*.

Nine Practices

1. Founded within the Christian mystical tradition, Centering Prayer was formalized into this prayer method by three Trappist monks: Fathers Basil Pennington, William Menninger, and Thomas Keating. I find it to be an extraordinarily egalitarian and unifying practice available to us irrespective of faith background, financial resources, geography, athleticism, and so on. In fact, in our Evolving Enneagram community, our faculty leads

groups of individuals who identify as Christian, Muslim, Jewish, "spiritual but not religious," pagan, Buddhist, and more—all sharing in sacred circle joined by this practice.

2. Bourgeault, *Centering Prayer and Inner Awakening*, 81.
3. Bourgeault, *Centering Prayer and Inner Awakening*, 5.
4. Keating, *Open Mind, Open Heart*, 22.
5. Bourgeault, *Centering Prayer and Inner Awakening*, 9.
6. See Contemplative Outreach, "Centering Prayer."
7. Welcoming Prayer was developed in 1983 by Mary Mrozowski, one of the founders of Contemplative Outreach. You can find the original practice on the Contemplative Outreach webpage (www.contemplativeoutreach.org). The following is my adapted version of it, which I personally practice as well as guide others in practicing in my one-on-one and group contemplative Enneagram work.
8. It is important to note here that this practice is for everyday triggers. If you have experienced a traumatic event, please consult a trauma specialist who can support you in allowing your feelings to move through you without retraumatizing you.
9. Bourgeault, *Centering Prayer and Inner Awakening*, 135.
10. Bourgeault, *Centering Prayer and Inner Awakening*, 146.
11. Our Enneagram type can be defined based on the prevalence of one core emotional habit (aka the type's "vice" or "passion") and one core mental habit (aka the type's "fixation"). See Appendix B for a few great books on this topic.
12. Beattie, *Language of Letting Go*, 214.
13. *Spiritual bypassing* is a term coined by Buddhist teacher John Welwood. Essentially, it is the act of using spiritual beliefs to avoid facing or healing one's painful feelings, unresolved wounds, and unmet needs. It is a state of avoidance and, as such, it is a state of resisting truth under the guise of maintaining a "spiritual" persona.
14. Excerpted from Rohr, "Gratitude and Generosity."
15. I want to acknowledge the power of wonder in our lives as well and imagine that this practice will bring forth both awe and wonder. However, I am conscious of an important distinction renowned researcher and author Brené Brown made between the two in her lexicon of emotions and experiences in *Atlas of the Heart*. According to Brown, awe occurs when we "stand back and observe to provide a stage for the phenomenon to shine." Wonder, while similar, inspires in us a wish to also understand. This awe practice focuses on the step that does not involve leaning forward to understand—even if and when we are inclined that way (especially those of us who are Enneagram head types: Types 5, 6, and 7). Rather than rush toward understanding and wondering, we might simply stay in our sense of bafflement.

16. Keltner, *Awe: New Science of Everyday Wonder*, 7.

17. Keltner, *Awe: New Science of Everyday Wonder*, xviii.

18. Keltner, *Awe: New Science of Everyday Wonder*, 106.

19. Cole Arthur Riley, *This Here Flesh*, 31.

20. Pilar, "What Is The Meaning of Anjali Mudra?"

21. Rea, "What Is Anjali Mudra?"

22. Mohan with Mohan, "Memories of a Master."

23. Rea, "What Is Anjali Mudra?"

24. If you cannot comfortably do this, please be gentle with yourself, start where you are physically and focus on the spirit of this practice, which is about honoring the wholeness and holiness of all life, including yours!

25. Goldberg, *Writing Down the Bones*, 66.

26. Goldberg, *True Secret of Writing*, 20.

27. Unity's method of Affirmative Prayer is sometimes called Positive Prayer. While many great Unity prayer resources reference "Positive Prayer," I prefer to call this prayer method "Affirmative Prayer" because the term *positive* can cause people to incorrectly interpret it as the same thing as positive or even magical thinking, which too often suggests a denial of our experience in favor of a positive reframe, or it perpetuates the misunderstanding that if we think or believe in something earnestly enough, we can cause it to manifest in the world.

28. Unity, "About Affirmative Prayer."

29. Unity, "Unity Five-Step Prayer Process."

Part II: Forty Activations

1. In these activations, "e" followed by the numeral stands for "Enneagram type [number]."

2. Bowen and Marlatt, "Surfing the Urge," 666–71.

3. © 2023, Pathways of Light. http://www.pathwaysoflight.org (commentary on *A Course in Miracles*, W-254).

4. Pathways of Light.

5. Heuertz, *Sacred Enneagram*, 229.

6. I learned this term from one of my first Enneagram teachers, Peter O'Hanrahan, Faculty at TNE.

7. As a reminder, type is used to refer to the nine distinct personality types on the Enneagram. When we are referring to the Enneagram as a map (e.g., a typography of my conscious development), it is more accurate to say, for example, "I embodied qualities attributed to point 9 (which are not exclusive to those who identify with Type 9) on the map of consciousness."

Appendix A: Evolving Together: A Guide for Groups

1. These are based on the group guidelines that my contemplative Enneagram groups have been using in our weekly gatherings since 2017. For detailed information about the guidelines, visit www.evolvingenneagram.com. Although some of these guidelines might feel overly strict or formal at first glance, we have found that, when devotedly applied, they help to foster an exceptionally safe and brave space for connecting, soul to soul, in ways most of us don't get to do in other spaces.

2. In our contemplative Enneagram groups, I've found that the "no unsolicited advice" guideline empowers individuals to discern their own truth and to ask for others' counsel only when they want it, which we find happens less frequently than one might expect. I often say: if you are fully present with someone and just let them talk, they will ramble their way into wisdom. Most of the time, in regular discourse, when someone appears to be struggling, we jump in, eager to help too hastily with our own undoubtedly sage advice—and a box of tissues. However, in most cases, creating a safe space for this work really means holding sacred silence as the other person's inner wisdom emerges, rather than interrupting their process with our impulse to help. In our contemplative practice circles, we do not even pass the tissue box when someone is crying unless and until they themselves start to look for tissues or ask for them. The offer to help can derail a person's process, especially if they do not have easy access to their own feelings or tears. Literally but also symbolically, in this small gesture of not passing the tissue, we make space for a person to cry out more fully the tears they may have long waited to shed.

3. For groups newer to the silence, you can try starting with ten minutes. However, I highly recommend you not skip the practice in favor for more sharing.

4. To be clear, I do believe gifted individuals out there might be amazing non-credentialed Enneagram practitioners. Unfortunately, access to the funding or time needed to certify or become accredited still varies by demographic and there are still underrepresented populations among Enneagram professionals (though progress seems to be being made). Conversely, being "certified" or "accredited" certainly does not guarantee someone is an excellent Enneagram mentor. Still, it might help you in your vetting process to know that to become an International Enneagram Association (IEA) Accredited Professional, a person needs to meet certain experiential, educational, and ethical criteria as well as have recommendations from teachers and peers. "Certification" is different and relates to whether a person has completed a specific program for competency within an Enneagram school—ideally through a school or teacher who is IEA-Accredited.

ABOUT THE AUTHOR

Founder of Evolving Enneagram, Reverend Nhien Vuong, JD, MDiv, is an international Enneagram presenter and retreat leader, contemplative community builder, and transformational soul guide. Nhien has been studying the Enneagram since 2002 and teaching it since 2007. She earned the IEA Accredited Professional with Distinction mark in 2024 and is certified in both the Somatic Enneagram and the IEA-Accredited Awareness to Action program. Nhien has presented professionally in countries including Egypt, the United States, Mexico, Denmark, and Sweden and at online global summits that have reached upwards of forty thousand people in over one hundred and fifty countries.

An ordained Unity minister, Nhien is best known for her work nurturing sacred inter-spiritual, Enneagram-literate spaces for individuals to cultivate authenticity, wholeness, and belonging. She regularly offers scholarships for Evolving Enneagram's many transformational programs and donates her time to various nonprofits and the incarcerated. Nhien's personal vision is for a more compassionate, awakened, and unified world.

This is where you can find out more about Nhien, her community, her writings, and her work:

www.evolvingenneagram.com

nhien-vuong.com

YouTube: @evolvingenneagram

Instagram: @evolvingenneagram

Facebook Business Page: Evolving Enneagram

Facebook Community Page: Evolving Enneagram Community

LinkedIn: Nhien Vuong

Insight Timer App: Evolving Enneagram

TO OUR READERS

Hampton Roads Publishing, an imprint of Red Wheel/Weiser, publishes inspirational books from a variety of spiritual traditions and philosophical perspectives for "the evolving human spirit."

Our readers are our most important resource, and we appreciate your input, suggestions, and ideas about what you would like to see published.

Visit our website at *www.redwheelweiser.com*, where you can learn about our upcoming books and also find links to sign up for our newsletter and exclusive offers.

You can also contact us at *info@rwwbooks.com* or at

Red Wheel/Weiser, LLC
65 Parker Street, Suite 7
Newburyport, MA 01950